The Pulse of Life

By Edward Esko

One Peaceful World Press
Becket, Massachusetts

Published by One Peaceful World, Becket, Massachusetts, U.S.A.

For further information on mail-order sales, wholesale or retail discounts,
distribution, translations, and foreign rights, please contact the publisher:

One Peaceful World Press
P.O. Box 10
308 Leland Road
Becket, MA 01223
U.S.A.

Telephone (413) 623-2322
Fax (413) 623-8827

First Edition: February 1994
10 9 8 7 6 5 4 3 2 1

ISBN 1–882984–05–6
Printed in U.S.A.

Introduction

This past October, the macrobiotic community around the world celebrated the hundredth anniversary of George Ohsawa's birth. Mr. Ohsawa was born in Japan and was the founder of the modern macrobiotic movement. The year 1993 marked the end of the first century of modern macrobiotics and the beginning of a new era.

In the world at large, medical science and the general public have started to look more closely at macrobiotics. An article on the macrobiotic approach to cancer was published in the *Journal of the American College of Nutrition* (Volume 12, No. 3, 205-208, 1993). The article is by Dr. James Carter of the Tulane University Medical Center and associates and reported on the experience of patients with pancreatic, metastatic prostate, and other forms of cancer who practiced macrobiotics. According to the report, "the macrobiotic diet seems to prevent tumor growth," and these findings "raise the important question of whether dietary modification may be effective adjunctive treatment to either chemotherapy/radiation therapy and/or surgery, substitution therapy for those refusing standard treatment, or in primary management of cancers whose etiologies have nutritional links..."

During the past twelve months, macrobiotics was featured on the *CBS Evening News*, Dr. Spock made worldwide headlines with his statement reconsidering the wisdom of feeding dairy food to babies and children, and Dr. Hugh Faulkner, author of *Physician Heal Thyself,* was profiled in *USA Today*. A survey was published in the *New England Journal of Medicine* stating that one-third of all Americans have sought help from alternative medicine, including macrobiotics.

At the Kushi Institute in Becket, construction started on a new building. The building will serve as a dormitory and teaching facility for the increasing number of students attending programs at the Institute. Kushi Institute extensions were held in San Francisco, Los Angeles, Toronto, Cleveland, and Philadelphia, and the K.I. faculty in Becket has been busy revising the curriculum for the Dynamics of Macrobiotics program. The new Level I curriculum was introduced in September to a group of about twenty full-time students. In August, the Kushi Foundation held its annual Macrobiotic Summer Conference in Vermont. Over 750 people attended, making the 1993 conference the biggest one so far. Meanwhile, hundreds of people from throughout the United States and Canada, and from as far away as Singapore, the Philippines, and Taiwan, attended the popular Way to Health program at the Institute. Along with teaching in Becket, during the past year my personal schedule took me to California, Florida, New York State, Toronto, Michigan, South Carolina, Virginia, Rhode Island, Pennsylvania, Cape Cod, Washington, D.C., the United Nations in New York, and London and Brussels.

In the midst of these activities, I somehow managed to prepare several new books for publication, which along with this one, include Michio Kushi's *Holistic Health Through Macrobiotics*, *Healing Harvest*, *Spiritual Journey*, and a revised edition of *Macrobiotic Child Care*. This second volume of essays follows *Notes from the Boundless Frontier*, published last year by One Peaceful World Press. In selecting the essays for the book, I have tried to achieve a balance of yin and yang, by including old and new material, articles that deal with personal experiences and those which explore the social application of macrobiotics, and articles with a more practical focus and those with a more theoretical slant.

I would like to thank everyone who inspired and helped in the completion of this book, including macrobiotic teachers such as George and Lima Ohsawa, Michio and Aveline Kushi, and Herman and Cornelia Aihara, my associates at the Kushi Institute and around the world, and the thousands of students and friends I have met over the years. I thank Alex and Gale Jack for supervising production and copyediting, George Wiel for help with production, and Bettina Zumdick for the wonderful illustrations. I also thank Carry Wolf and Berta Schurmann for their support, and Wendy and the children for their love, inspiration, and encouragement.

Edward Esko
Becket, Massachusetts
December, 1993

Contents

Part I: Personal Adventures

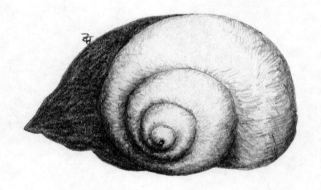

1. Europe 1977

In October, 1977 I accompanied Michio and Aveline Kushi on a tour of several European cities. The trip lasted for five weeks and included stops in Paris, Amsterdam, London, and Ghent. It was the first of many trips to Europe, and offered a unique opportunity to participate in the early development of macrobiotics on the other side of the Atlantic.

Paris

While crossing the Atlantic on the way to Paris, Michio showed me a letter he received from a group of people who wanted to organize a European Macrobiotic Congress in the autumn of 1978. Our first meeting in Paris would be with this group to discuss ideas about the congress. Following that, Michio was scheduled to give several lectures and Aveline several cooking classes.

We were met at the airport by several of the friends who were arranging Michio's seminar. After settling into our respective lodgings in the city, we met for dinner at macrobiotic restaurant named the Four Oceans. On the following day I joined the Kushis and several friends for lunch at the Tenryu Institute, a macrobiotic study center founded by a woman named Francios Riviere. For many years, Madame Riviere had been a student of George Ohsawa. After lunch, she led us into her office. She lit a stick of incense and placed it in front of a small shrine dedicated to Mr. Ohsawa. Everyone joined her in offering thanks to this great teacher.

The next day we met with a small group of people from France, Belgium, Germany, England, and Switzerland in order to discuss the European Congress. In addition to the Kushis, senior macrobiotic people such as Clim Yoshime from Belgium, Jiro Nakamura from Germany (both of whom had studied with George Ohsawa), and Bill Tara were in attendance. After lunch at a macrobiotic restaurant named Le Bol en Bois (the Wooden Bowl), the meeting adjourned.

The first European Macrobiotic Assembly took place the following year at the Community Health Foundation in London. It was attended by Lima Ohsawa, Michio and Aveline Kushi, Herman Aihara, and macrobiotic people from throughout Europe. It was followed by the first North American Macrobiotic Congress, which took place in Boston in 1979.

Michio's lecture, titled *The Universal Way of Health*, was held in a large auditorium in the center of Paris. The hall had a seating capacity of about 500, and when the lecture began, there were no seats left. Michio's seminars were organized by the European Macrobiotic Union, an association of macrobiotic centers in France. On the following day, we were faced with the problem of not enough space. The hall booked for the weekend seminar had a seating capacity of 200. Those spaces were filled several days before, and unfortunately another 200 people had to be turned away. In any case, the people who attended enjoyed studies on Oriental medicine, spiritual development, human destiny, and other fascinating topics.

Amsterdam

In 1977, macrobiotic activities in Holland were coordinated by the East West Center, or Oost West Centrum. The East West Center was founded by Adelbert and Weike Nelissen, and had recently moved to a large building in the center of the city. On the first floor of the building was a large hall with space for several hundred people, next to which were administrative offices. On the second floor were kitchen facilities, several small classrooms, and a dining area. The upper floor of the building had been converted into apartments where several staff members were staying.

This was Michio and Aveline's fourth visit to Amsterdam. The seminar took place over six days, and was divided into three sessions. The first session took place on a weekend, and featured an introduction to macrobiotics and Oriental medicine, along with cooking classes. The other sessions focused on spiritual development. During our visit, a store offering macrobiotic foods opened in the center. Adelbert mentioned that this was the fifth natural food store to open in Amsterdam, and that about 500 stores were offering macrobiotic products throughout Holland.

London

The East West Center in London was started in January, 1977 by Bill Tara and friends. Bill had studied with Michio in the Sixties and moved to England to establish a macrobiotic educational center. The center is located in a large building near St. Paul's Cathedral, and houses the Community Health Foundation (CHF), a non-profit educational organization. The Foundation offers regular lectures, seminars, and workshops on various aspects of macrobiotics, including classes presented by the resident staff and workshops by visiting teachers. Many people visit the center for macrobiotic counseling and shiatsu. The center buzzes with activity from morning until night.

Michio's lectures were held in the CHF's conference center. This was his fifth visit to London in two years, and the third time his classes were held at the CHF. Michio also met with the students at the Kushi Institute. About twenty-five people were enrolled in that first Level I program established for people who wanted to become macrobiotic teachers and counselors. I also had the opportunity to lecture at the K.I., and found the students to be highly motivated and sincere. The Institute started the following year in Boston to fill the need for macrobiotic teachers in North America.

Sunwheel Foods, which at that time was the leading distributor of macrobiotic staples in Britain, was one of the many enterprises associated with the center. It was started in 1974 by Bill Tara and Peter Bradford, and was actively distributing macrobiotic foods to over 300 stores throughout the U.K. Several large health food chains were also distributing macrobiotic products to another 700 stores. Bill Tara told me that whole foods were becoming increasingly popular in Britain.

Ghent

Many of the macrobiotic traditions of old Europe are still apparent in Belgium. In the center of Ghent is a large market known as the *Koornmarkt*. In Flemish, the word *koorn* means grain. Next to it is a market that specializes in vegetables. Both landmarks have been there since the Middle Ages. This environment provided an appropriate backdrop for the first International Macrobiotic Fair.

The fair was held in a large convention center in Ghent. The building was filled with booths of various sorts, ranging from displays of natural crafts and furniture to concessions selling a variety of natural foods. The opening ceremony took place in a large auditorium. Marc Van Cauwenberghe, my colleague from Boston, spoke first and read a message from Michio and Aveline. (The Kushis had returned to Boston after the seminar in London.) In attendance were friends from macrobiotic centers in other countries, members of the press, and a delegation sent by the mayor.

On the second day of the fair, I lectured in the auditorium. I reported on the East West Foundation's cancer and diet programs, and predicted that macrobiotic health care would become increasingly sought after in the near future. I also mentioned that a growing number of doctors were becoming interested in macrobiotics. Several hundred people attended the lecture. The last day of the fair was a Sunday, and was the most crowded of the three-day event. About 10,000 people had come to the fair; most who attended were new to macrobiotics. The International Macrobiotic Fair had been a success!

Going to Europe with the Kushis gave me a different perspective on the worldwide development of macrobiotics. The trip also brought me closer to macrobiotic traditions in the West. By 1977, Michio's European seminars had become major international events; participating in them gave me the feeling that we were making history. I found the macrobiotic movement in Europe brimming with energy and vitality. It will no doubt grow, develop, and inspire the whole world in the future.

Source: This essay is based on an article entitled, *Macrobiotics in Europe*, published in *Order of the Universe*, Boston, Mass., 1978.

2. Riding the Night Owl

At about 9:30, the waiting area in Union Station begins to fill with people waiting to board the Night Owl. The train leaves Washington every night at 10:10, arriving at Back Bay Station in Boston the following morning. During the night, it makes stops in Baltimore, Philadelphia, and New York, and at stations in Connecticut and Rhode Island.

Thirty minutes later, the green door leading to the platform opens. A voice on the loudspeaker announces that the Night Owl is ready for boarding. Wendy, the children, and I step out of the air-conditioned station and into the hot July night. We are returning home to Boston after giving lectures and visiting friends in Philadelphia and Washington. It has been a busy summer. Not only have we traveled down the East Coast for lectures, but have been busily engaged in preparing for the 1978 Amherst Summer Program, made special this year by a visit from Lima Ohsawa.

Since the children were accompanying us on the trip, we decided against riding coach and booked a sleeping compartment instead. The compartment is small, but comfortable. It has fold-out beds that double as couches. As we settle into our quarters, the train begins to pull out of the station. Washington begins to pass by the window, at first slowly, and then quickly, as then disappears as we enter the Maryland countryside. Soon Wendy and the children are asleep.

Sitting by the window, I think of a recent article about scientists who had come up with an experiment designed to bring us closer to a unified field theory. It seems that the present understanding of electromagnetism, gravity, and the motion of subatomic particles contains contradictions that require a unified theory to resolve.

Fortunately, humanity doesn't have to wait for science to discover the principle of life. We already possess the unifying principle and have seen it work a thousand miracles, including recovery from so-called "incurable" diseases. George Ohsawa, Michio Kushi, Herman Aihara, and other teachers have explored its applications in a thousand domains. We are already enjoying the principle of life that science is trying to discover. What an incredible adventure it is to have this principle and to be using it on a daily basis.

Out of nowhere comes a knock at the door. "Tickets, please!" I open the door and hand our tickets to the conductor. Soon, streets lined with row houses announce our arrival in Baltimore. The train slows down and stops at the station.

As the train picks up speed after making the stop, I become aware that its motion is a reflection of the order of the universe. It does not pass over the tracks in a straight line but glides over the rails in a subtle up and down, or waving motion. That, plus the gentle rocking of the train from side to side, produces a feeling of well-being and security. I realize that we are constantly moving through the universe at incredible speed. Like the train, this motion takes the form of waves that alternate between two opposite tendencies—yin and yang, expansion and contraction, up and down. I realize that yin and yang can only be understood in terms of the dynamic movement of energy. As soon as we lock them into a static concept, they lose their essence, which is movement itself, and become meaningless.

Since ancient times, sages have advised humanity to follow the middle way. Keeping a moderate balance of yin and yang in our diet and daily life leads to health and happiness. By keeping reasonably close to a central line of balance, we pursue the line of least resistance in our movement through life. The result is physical and mental health. Sickness and unhappiness result when we follow extremes. The further we move from the line of balance, the more we encounter friction, which takes the form of sickness and unhappiness.

From the moving train, the changing scenes outside the window appear like changing images on a movie screen. While the train is moving, it is impossible to isolate any one of the successive images that come into view for a moment, only to be replaced by a new image. I am at once struck by their ephemerality. The only constant is movement and change.

Herein lies another key to human happiness. We are constantly moving into new and uncharted territory. Happiness arises from the joyful adaptation to these changes. Unhappiness results when we forget that life is a continual process of change and become stuck and attached. This arises because of internal stagnation. Stagnation can happen very easily if we are eating too much sugar, fat, cheese, milk, and other foods that cause our blood condition to become sticky or that weaken our vitality and make us lose the desire to pursue our dream. The solution to this is to return to the line of least resistance through proper eating, physical activity, and self-reflection.

Somewhere between Baltimore and Philadelphia, we pass a body of water that, off in the darkness, appears quite large. I assume it is the upper Chesapeake Bay. The night is foggy and there is a mist over the dark water. It is difficult to tell where the water leaves off and the sky begins. Meanwhile, off in the distance, tiny lights are flickering. Perhaps they are the lights of a fishing boat or a buoy.

The darkness over the bay is like the infinite expanse of the universe, without form and boundless. The tiny, flickering lights are like universes that appear, disappear, and re-emerge in new form within the boundless ocean of infinity. Science is aware that the universe is expanding endlessly. Beyond the most distant galaxies, astronomers have discovered a source of radio waves they believe to be the background of the universe. They envision it as a cloud of preatomic particles that surrounds the universe, something like the cloud of comets that surrounds the solar system.

The logarithmic spiral taught by George Ohsawa enables us to understand this discovery. It explains the creation of the universe from the world of infinity—beyond time and space, beyond the distinctions of the relative world—through the appearance of yin and yang, vibrations, preatomic particles, elements, vegetation, and animal life, including man. This seven-staged process is symbolized in the Book of Genesis. The part of the universe we can see or detect is ultimately tiny in comparison to the invisible part that exists beyond the senses. Preatomic particles, like those discovered by astronomers at the periphery of the universe, occupy the fourth orbit of the spiral. They exist both beyond and within the world of matter. They are, in turn, the product of pure energy; the vibrations of pure energy are, in turn, produced by yin and yang, the primary forces of expansion and contraction that arise within the infinite oneness.

Our universe is like one of the tiny lights that flicker off and on within the surrounding mist. It is one of countless other spiral universes; each represented by a flickering light. The dark, misty water seems without beginning or end; like the world of infinity itself.

Our life on earth is short in comparison to the life of the universe. Yet the universe exists only as a brief flicker within the infinite ocean of time and space. Our true identity is the infinite universe itself, beyond the relative ever-changing world. As the train continues northward, I feel a deep sense of gratitude toward macrobiotics for giving me a glimpse of this infinite world and humanity's true identity.

Source: This essay is based on an article entitled, *Riding the Night Owl: An Essay on Movement and Change*, published in *The Macrobiotic*, Number 127, Oroville, Ca., December, 1978.

Relativity

Last winter, I visited Long Island for lectures. Two weeks later, I taught in Southern California. In both places, I took a walk by the ocean. The contrast offered an interesting study in yin and yang. On Long Island, a cold wind whipped across the shore; while in Southern California, the breeze was warm and gentle. On Long Island, the colors were subdued; in Southern California, they were brilliant and stunning. On Long Island, I huddled to keep warm, while in Southern California, we took off our shoes and walked barefoot on the sand. On Long Island, I walked briskly; in Southern California, we adopted a leisurely pace. It was difficult to spend more than ten minutes at the beach on Long Island, while in Southern California, we could have easily spent the whole day. On Long Island, the effect was bracing; in Southern California, it was relaxing. We are conditioned by our environment; we become more yin or more yang in response to environmental conditions.

3. The Quest for Peace

In each and every country
And each and every land,
The people of our planet
Will start to understand,
That we can live together
In peace and harmony,
And love will grow between us
Like one big family.
   —One Peaceful World Song

In the early 1980s, the international political situation was becoming increasingly tense. Dark clouds of war were appearing on the horizon. The Soviet Union had just invaded Afghanistan and the United States was gearing up for the largest military buildup in its history. Michio and Aveline Kushi went on a lecture tour of Europe that included a stop in West Berlin. When they returned to Boston, they reported on the increasing tension there and the high level of concern throughout Europe about the possibility of war. Michio stated that in his opinion, unless the situation changed, there was a 90 percent chance of a nuclear war occurring during the 1980s.

To underscore his concern, in June, 1980, Michio presented a special lecture on the possibility of war. He invited the fire chief of Lawrence, Massachusetts, to report on the damage that would occur if Boston were hit with a nuclear bomb. The lecture had a sobering effect on everyone. It alerted me to the urgency of focusing on the issue of world peace in my writings, lectures, and social contacts.

Soon after the lecture, I began contacting leaders in the disarmament movement. My idea was to present the macrobiotic approach as a model for personal and planetary healing. My hope was to stimulate new thinking about the possibility of achieving world peace.

The differences between the United States and the Soviet Union that were threatening to trigger war were caused by a hardening or rigidity of thinking on both sides, leading to increasing polarization. Ideological rigidity is the result of physical hardening and rigidity produced by an unbalanced diet, especially the overconsumption of animal food. Eating whole grains and vegetables dissolves mental and physical inflexibility and makes it easier for two sides to compromise and arrive at a harmonious resolution of their differences.

One of the first people I went to see was the president of the Union of Concerned Scientists. He was also the head of the department of nuclear physics at MIT. The Union of Concerned Scientists is made up of scientists from around the world who are concerned about the spread of nuclear technology and the threat of nuclear war. During our meeting, I explained how macrobiotics had changed the dietary habits of many people throughout the world and offered a potential solution to degenerative disease and war. Although he appreciated my views, he felt that political leaders would not change until a worldwide consensus pressured them to.

I also met with representatives of Physicians for Social Responsibility (PSR), an international group of doctors (which had members in the USSR) concerned with the medical consequences of nuclear war. Twenty years earlier, PSR had conducted a study of the consequences of a nuclear strike on the city of Boston. The results of that study, which showed that a nuclear attack would destroy most of the city, made a deep impression on President Kennedy. The study motivated Kennedy to propose and later sign a nuclear test ban treaty with Kruschev, an act considered by many to be a turning point in the Cold War.

The doctors were of the opinion that nuclear war would be a public health disaster of unprecedented magnitude that would overwhelm the capability of the medical profession to respond. Since there could be no effective medical response to such a catastrophe, the doctors felt that prevention was the only sane option. They had updated their study on the effects of a nuclear strike on Boston, showing how the more powerful weapons of the 1980s would cause an unimaginable degree of devastation. Their position was that once a nuclear war started, there was no way it would remain "limited," or could in any way be considered "winnable," since both sides would be destroyed. The doctors believed that only a worldwide call for nuclear disarmament would change the official policies of both superpowers.

During the meeting with members of PSR, it was suggested that representatives from the macrobiotic community attend a reception for a Soviet peace delegation at the home of Dr. Helen Caldicott. Dr. Caldicott is a pediatrician from Australia who gained international prominence for her work for nuclear disarmament. She was hosting a reception at which members of the Supreme Soviet, the equivalent of the Soviet parliament, would be in attendance. The reception was held on a Sunday afternoon at Dr. Caldicott's home in Newton, Massachusetts. Several hundred people were in attendance, including the ten-member Soviet delegation and camera crews from Boston television stations.

Dr. Caldicott's reception offered an unexpected opportunity to present our views to representatives of the Soviet Government. In preparation for the meeting, the members of our group, Tom Monte, Tim Goodwin, and Janet Lacy, compiled a packet of information for each of the Soviets. The packets included *Cancer and Diet*, a booklet published by the East West Foundation, and a letter explaining the macrobiotic approach to planetary health and peace. During the reception, we handed a packet to each of the Soviets while asking them questions such as, "What is the current rate of cancer in the USSR?", "How has the Soviet diet changed in the past forty years?", "Do you know of any research in your country linking diet with degenerative disease?", and "Do you think a diet of whole grains and vegetables would make people less inclined to war and more open to pursuing a peaceful resolution to their differences?"

The Soviets were surprised by the nature of our questioning and were unable to provide answers. However they thanked us for the materials. One younger member of the delegation told us he would pass our information on to the minister of health in his country.

World Health, World Peace

Meanwhile, under Michio's guidance, the East West Foundation decided to make "World Health-World Peace" the theme of its educational events in Boston. This theme was adopted by the 1982 North American Macrobiotic Congress that was attended by over 100 delegates from throughout the

19

United States and Canada. During the Congress, the committee I chaired drafted a series of precepts for peace based on the Seven Universal Principles of the Order of the Universe. The Seven Precepts for World Peace were published in the report issued by the Congress, and later in the book, *One Peaceful World*, by Michio Kushi and Alex Jack (St. Martin's Press, 1987). The Seven Precepts are as follows:

1. All people live on one planet, the earth.
2. The current world crisis offers an opportunity to achieve lasting peace.
3. All ways of life complement each other and contribute to overall harmony and balance.
4. Modern humanity has a unique opportunity to establish lasting peace.
5. The possibility of global war coexists with the opportunity for global peace.
6. The greater the threat of war and destruction, the greater the need for international cooperation and communication.
7. The development of nuclear weapons has made war obsolete; thus the era of one peaceful world is now beginning.

These precepts are derived from the Seven Universal Principles of the Infinite Universe.

1. Everything is a differentiation of one infinity.
2. Everything changes.
3. All antagonisms are complementary.
4. There is nothing identical.
5. What has a front has a back.
6. The bigger the front, the bigger the back.
7. What has a beginning has an end.

Together with the work of groups such as the Union of Concerned Scientists and Physicians for Social Responsibility, these efforts produced ripples that spiraled out far beyond Boston. Eventually, the call for nuclear disarmament and an end to superpower conflict became a global mandate that influenced both the White House and the Kremlin. Within several years, Ronald Reagan and Mikhail Gorbachev were negotiating deep cuts in the nuclear arsenals of both superpowers. By the end of the decade, the Berlin Wall fell and the Cold War faded into history. For the time being, it seemed the possibility of nuclear war had been averted.

One Peaceful World Studies at the Kushi Institute

Together with working for the immediate goal of preventing war, it became apparent that we needed to study the issue of world federation as a constructive, long-term solution. I began a program of world peace studies at the Kushi Institute. In 1983, I reported on these activities in a letter to the North American Macrobiotic Congress:

One of the proposals discussed during the 1982 North American Macrobiotic Congress was to encourage courses or lectures on the subjects of world peace and world federation at macrobiotic centers throughout the world. Over the past year, regular studies on these subjects have been presented as a part of the Level III course on the Order of the Universe at the Kushi Institute. These studies have covered the following:

1. The background to one peaceful world, including celestial and historical cycles.
2. Macrobiotics as the biological foundation for future world federation.
3. A review of past and present utopian models and proposals for world peace, including *Perpetual Peace* by Immanuel Kant, *Utopia* by Thomas Moore, *Erewhon* by Samuel Butler, the Charter of the League of Nations and the United Nations Charter, Albert Einstein's *Ideas and Opinions*, *The Fate of the Earth*, an excellent book by Jonathan Schell published in 1982, and the *Preliminary Draft of a World Constitution*, prepared after the Second World War by Robert Hutchins and others at the University of Chicago.

Each of the students in these classes selected one of these proposals and presented a ten minute oral report, commenting on the strong and weak points of each, and relevance of each to our present situation.
4. Original proposals for world peace. Following the review of past world peace proposals, the students were asked to make a brief report on their ideas for realizing the dream

of world peace and world federation, followed by questions and discussion.

During the class, various study materials were distributed, including astronomical charts, such as those showing the celestial cycles that influence the movement of history; the Seven Precepts for World Peace drafted by the 1982 Macrobiotic Congress, and quotations from various thinkers about the need for world federation, including Dostoevsky, Kant, Dante, and the English historian, Arnold Toynbee. Epictetus, the Greek philosopher often quoted by George Ohsawa ("If a man is unhappy, it is his own fault"), stated:

> There is but one course open to men, to do as Socrates did: never to reply to one who asks his country, "I am Athenian," or "I am Corinthian," but "I am a citizen of the universe."

The education committee has made copies of these study materials available for use in your center, should you decide to include world peace and related subjects in your educational program. Feel free to distribute these materials to students who participate in your lectures or classes. Copies of the *Preliminary Draft of a World Constitution*, which may serve as a starting point for the creation of a future world macrobiotic constitution, can also be made available to you.

War in the Persian Gulf

As the 1990s began, the clouds of war reappeared on the horizon, this time, in the Middle East. The Persian Gulf War represented a different type of conflict. The macrobiotic response was also different, and started to be initiated by a new generation. My eldest son, Eric became active in the quest for a peaceful solution in the Middle East, as did others of his generation. Eric wrote the following article for the *One Peaceful World* newsletter:

> My name is Eric Esko. My parents are teachers of macrobiotics in Becket, Massachusetts. Like many people my age, I am concerned about the future of the world. Of the many threats facing humanity in the 1990s, the threat of war is

one of the most serious. Ever since I can remember, my family would get together to sing the *One Peaceful World* song. I realized that macrobiotics and world peace go hand in hand, and are in fact the same thing.

In an age of nuclear weapons, humanity will eventually become extinct unless we find a way of living together peacefully. The first step toward peace is to eliminate all machines of death and destruction. Then we must take a look at our way of eating. Killing animals for food is not necessary unless foods such as grains and vegetables are not available. Grains and vegetables are abundant throughout the world, so eating animal food is largely unnecessary. Instead of trying to destroy countries we think of as undesirable, we should help them as much as possible until they become peaceful. One of the biggest problems preventing world peace is world hunger. To stop that we must stop relying on animal food and educate ourselves in natural farming so that we can become more self-sufficient. When these problems are solved, we will be one step closer to world peace.

The crisis in the Middle East has erupted into a destructive war. It is an impediment to our progress toward one peaceful world. It is important for macrobiotic people, and especially the young generation, to speak out and point the way toward world peace. In December, 1990, several macrobiotic friends and I participated in a candlelight vigil for peace held in Amherst, Massachusetts, not far from my home in Becket. About 300 people—each with a lit candle—formed a large circle and stood in mediation for a half-hour in the center of the town. We also signed a petition asking President Bush to search for a peaceful solution in the Middle East. The petition was later sent to the White House.

I would like to hear from other young people who share these views. I hope to set up a network of young people committed to world peace. I think it is important for those of us who share the dream of macrobiotics and world peace to communicate and stay in touch. Please write to me if you are interested in sharing your ideas.

Waterloo

In the spring of 1993 I visited England and Belgium for lectures. I arrived first in London, where I gave a weekend seminar at the Community Health Foundation. While in London, I met with leaders in the macrobiotic movement in Britain, including Jon Sandifer, Peter Bradford, Donald Cox, and Simon Brown. I also met with Denny and Melanie Waxman, who were visiting from their home in Portugal. I stayed at a small apartment being rented by two young women from the former Yugoslavia, one from Serbia and the other from Croatia, both of whom are practicing the macrobiotic way of life. Although their countries were recently at war, there was no sign of conflict between them. United by a common dream of health and peace, these two women are like sisters, not adversaries.

Ten minutes into my Saturday morning lecture, an explosion shook the five-story CHF building, rattling windows and blowing open the front door. A terrorist bomb had been set off in London's nearby financial district. The one-ton bomb shattered windows and caused a great deal of damage. After a minute or two, I continued the lecture. Interestingly, the bomb had been made from nitrogen fertilizer, providing yet another reason to support organic farming.

The energy in Belgium was more relaxed than that in London. It was late April, yet summer had already started. Everywhere, soft green colors greeted the eye. The weather was warm and sunny. Island nations such as Great Britain and Japan are surrounded by salt water, and this creates a very highly charged environment. A continent is by nature more open and expanded than an island. Fields, forests, and freshwater lakes are the primary natural influences, rather than the ocean.

I was met at the airport by Hanne Petersen. Originally from Copenhagen, Hanne lives with her parents outside Brussels. She completed all three levels of study at the Kushi Institute in Becket. After returning to Belgium, she took a job as a tour guide at EEC headquarters. Hanne had made arrangements for me to lecture in Brussels on the following evening.

The Petersens live in Rhode-Saint-Genese, next to the village of Waterloo, the site of Napoleon's defeat by the Duke of Wellington in 1815. Napoleon had suffered a major defeat the year before and exiled to the island of Elba, off the coast of Italy. However, being very yang (short, active, and stubborn), he escaped and raised another army. The final, decisive battle occurred at Waterloo, at which time the Napoleonic era came to an end.

The following day, Hanne and I drove to a beautiful wooded area not far from her home. Delightful blue flowers were blooming on the forest floor, creating a soft blue carpet that covered the ground beneath the trees. The afternoon sun shone through the forest canopy. An unexpectedly wonderful fragrance, more subtle than any perfume, permeated the air. The scene was alive with natural beauty.

On the way back to Rhode-Saint-Genese, we stopped at Waterloo. The site is now a national shrine, at the center of which is a hill with a large metal statue of a lion at the summit. Bullets and cannonballs were melted down and used to make the statue. In contrast to the tranquil beauty of the forest, I sensed agitation and sadness at Waterloo, as if the ghosts of the men who died in battle were still there. How many lives had perished in that place more than a century and a-half ago? Perhaps the day was as sunny and beautiful as the one we were enjoying. Suddenly, the struggles of men seem strangely out of synch with the enduring tranquility of nature.

Two days later, after bidding farewell to my kind hosts, I boarded an early morning train for Amsterdam, where I boarded a plane for Boston. As the train passed through the Flemish part of Belgium, the sun began to rise in East. Morning mist rose from the fields. I realized that in this century, these farms and villages had also seen epic battles. The morning mist seemed to carry the spirits of the young men who perished in these struggles. Once again, the futility of war was readily apparent.

The metal lion at Waterloo is symbolic of the underlying cause of such human tragedy. The lion is a carnivore and hunter. For him, a diet of meat is natural and appropriate. However, human beings are not lions. We have far greater intelligence and spiritual capacity. Unless we live in a polar climate, a diet high in animal food is against the natural order. When we base our diet on animal foods, our thinking and behavior start to resemble that of lions and tigers. Our senses become sharper, and we become impulsive, aggressive, and warlike. We become territorial, dividing the earth into artificial sections. Our range of perception narrows, and we lose sight of the peaceful natural order of which we are a part.

In the future, humanity will come to realize that the unifying principle of macrobiotics is actually the principle of peace and harmony. Through this principle, all conflicting factors are seen as complementary; all opposing forces can be brought together and harmonized. The negative tendencies that lead to war—fear, hostility, exclusivity, and intolerance—can be moderated and changed into their opposites. This process begins with a healthful natural diet based on the harmonious balance of yin and yang, or the energies of expansion and contraction. As the macrobiotic way of life spreads around the world, people will come to recognize that the common factors that unite us, such as humanity's universal tradition of eating grains and vegetables, are greater than the things that divide us. Our differences are actually complementary, and contribute to a greater harmony. The philosophy and practice of macrobiotics can bring about a world of genuine health and lasting peace.

Source: This essay is from personal notes and a letter to the 1983 North American Macrobiotic Congress. The article by Eric Esko is from *One Peaceful World*, Becket, Mass., Spring 1991, and *Macrobiotic Youth for Peace: Young People's Peace Network*, *MacroNews*, Philadelphia, Pa., January/February, 1991.

Peace Shrine Dedicated

Macrobiotic friends from Germany, Switzerland, and the United States dedicated a world peace shrine at Kirchholz in Dethighofen, Germany, on May 19, 1990. The shrine, modeled after the shrine for world peace in Becket, Mass., is intended to pacify the spirits and souls of all those who died from war and sickness in Europe through the ages. It is also intended as a place of spiritual purification and dedication to health and peace for all humanity in the future. Kirchholz is a beautiful mountain village near the border with Switzerland. It has been the site of numerous macrobiotic seminars and cooking intensives.

One Peaceful World Newsletter, *Summer, 1990*

4. With Dr. Spock in Maine

The coast of Maine has a special kind of charm. Unlike the gentle beaches one finds along the Mid-Atlantic coast where I was raised, the Maine coast is rugged and rocky. The people who inhabit the coast of Maine are strong and independently minded, Yankees in the truest sense of the word.

There are pockets of macrobiotic activity scattered throughout this huge state. Over the years I have lectured in Waldoboro, at the macrobiotic center started by John and Anna Ineson, in Portland, and at a spring retreat held at a beautiful lakeside resort in Damarascotta. John Ineson, an Episcopal minister and author of *The Way of Life: Macrobiotics and the Spirit of Christianity*, was at one time the interfaith chaplain at Colby College in Waterville. He arranged a macrobiotic symposium at Colby, at which I spoke, along with Alex Jack, Haruo Kushi, and several other macrobiotic teachers.

More recently, educational programs have centered around the town of Belfast, about two hours north of Portland along the coast. I was invited to to visit Belfast in June, 1992 by Elizabeth Masters and David Kingsbury. Together they manage Kingsbury House, a macrobiotic bed and breakfast in Belfast. Elizabeth is a graduate of the Kushi Institute. She turned to macrobiotics a number of years ago following a diagnosis of cancer. After recovering her health, she and David converted their large home into a cozy bed and breakfast, and began to sponsor potlucks and other macrobiotic activities.

Several weeks before the visit, I received a call from Mary Morgan. Mary is the wife of Dr. Benjamin Spock, the world renowned pediatrician, peace activist, and author of the classic *Baby and Child Care*. Dr. Spock had met another Kushi Institute teacher, Dr. Marc Van Cauwenberghe, the year before in Maine, and at the age of eighty-eight, started macrobiotics with Mary's support and encouragement. In an article in *USA Today*, Mary stated, "His health is my No.1 priority now, and I

27

think I've done a good job!" The article stated that Mary "orchestrates this thrice-weekly exercise sessions with a personal trainer, his daily 16 laps in a YMCA pool, and his weekly lessons with a macrobiotic chef."

Ben and Mary live part of the year in Camden, Maine, and part in Tortola, in the British Virgin Islands. Mary was calling from their summer home in Maine. She mentioned that she and Ben wanted to get together with me during my visit.

Earlier in the year, my wife, Wendy gave seminars in the Virgin Islands, and was invited by Ben and Mary to visit Tortola. Wendy enjoyed her visit tremendously, especially the time she spent in the kitchen showing Ben and Mary how to cut vegetables and prepare macrobiotic dishes. Following her return to Becket, she and I discussed inviting Dr. Spock to speak at the 1992 Macrobiotic Summer Conference in Vermont. Our friends at the Kushi Institute were enthusiastic about the idea and extended a formal invitation which Dr. Spock gladly accepted.

In preparation for our meeting, I read Dr. Spock's autobiography, *Spock On Spock* (Pantheon, 1985), which he and Mary co-authored. The book is appropriately subtitled, "A memoir of growing up with the century." Dr. Spock was born at the turn of the century, and has lived through two World Wars, the Great Depression, the Cold War, and the nuclear and space ages. All of the major events of the twentieth century are chronicled in his book, as are his meetings with many of the century's great personalities, including Charlie Chaplin and several U.S. presidents. In 1924, as a member of the Yale rowing team, Dr. Spock traveled to Paris to compete in the Olympics. Interestingly, during his voyage across the Atlantic, he met Gloria Swanson, the silent film star who like Dr. Spock, became macrobiotic later in life and participated in macrobiotic summer conferences and other educational programs.

After graduating from medical school, Dr. Spock trained in both pediatrics and psychiatry. (He was the first person in the country to train in both fields.) He established a practice in New York City during the Depression, and in the 1940s was approached by a publisher and asked to write a book. Thus *Baby and Child Care* came into being in 1945. The book became an overnight best-seller, and to date has sold 39 million copies. Dr. Spock's common sense advice about raising children reassured millions of parents and influenced the way an entire generation was brought up. (The book opens with the

line: "Trust yourself. You know more than you think you do.")
I consulted Dr. Spock's book on numerous occasions while
doing the research for *Macrobiotic Child Care and Family
Health*, which Wendy and I wrote with the Kushis in 1985.

In the late Fifties, Dr. Spock became active in the movement for nuclear disarmament and world peace. At the invitation of Homer Jack (Alex Jack's father), he joined the National
Committee for a Sane Nuclear Policy (SANE) in 1962. At that
time SANE was working principally for a nuclear test ban
treaty. As Dr. Spock states in his autobiography, he joined
SANE because he realized "that if we didn't have a test ban
treaty, more and more children, not only in America but around
the world, would die of cancer and leukemia or be born with
mental and physical defects from fallout radiation." It was Dr.
Spock's involvement with SANE that led to his well-publicized
involvement with the peace movement during the Sixties.

Elizabeth Masters had scheduled an introductory lecture on
Friday evening followed by an all-day workshop on the following day. The lectures were held in the hall of a large white
church typical of those found throughout New England. Ben
and Mary came to the evening lecture, and I invited them to
speak to the group of about thirty people who had gathered for
the talk. They gladly accepted, and explained how they discovered macrobiotics and how Ben had experienced immediate
improvements in his health.

I began the lecture by thanking Dr. Spock for his dedication
to world peace and the health and well-being of children
throughout the world. I mentioned that despite the end of the
Cold War, enormous problems still remained on the road to one
peaceful world. I stated my belief that macrobiotics offered a
long-term solution to problems of personal health and the environment, and a fundamental method for the creation of a
healthy and peaceful world. As I was speaking, I noticed Dr.
Spock nodding in approval.

On the following morning, I introduced the group to the ba-
sics of Oriental diagnosis. Ben and Mary participated in all of
the group discussions and practice sessions, and asked many
questions. They seemed to be thoroughly enjoying themselves.

I returned home on the following day. During the seven-
hour drive back to Becket, I reflected on my meeting with Dr.
Spock. I was impressed by Dr. Spock's youthful spirit and energy. At the age of eighty-nine, he is still seeking new knowledge and experience. His thinking is very flexible, and as a

physician, he is interested in learning about new approaches to health and well-being. His open-mindedness and enthusiasm exemplify the spirit of macrobiotics.

Dr. Spock influenced an entire generation, both through his common sense approach to child care and his dedication to peace. His embrace of macrobiotics could mean that the generation he guided will soon follow his lead and embrace a new and more healthy way of life.

Source: This essay is from personal notes, excerpts of which appeared in *Macrobiotics Today*, Oroville, Ca., November/December, 1992.

Macrobiotics at the United Nations

In September, 1992, the U.N. Macrobiotic Society met in New York to discuss the role of macrobiotics in personal health and the environment. The meeting featured a discussion with Edward Esko, author of Healing Planet Earth *(One Peaceful World Press, 1992.) The society was established in the 1980s by Katsuhide Kitatani, deputy executive director of the U.N. Population Fund, who recovered from stomach cancer through macrobiotics. Mr. Kitatani's story is told in the book,* Cancer-Free *(Japan Publications, 1992). The society is planning monthly lectures and events focusing on personal and planetary health through macrobiotics.*
One Peaceful World Newsletter, *Winter, 1993*

Part II: Creating a Healthy and Peaceful World

5. Misconceptions About Macrobiotics

In the 1970s, several articles appeared in national magazines in which the macrobiotic diet was labeled a dangerous fad diet. Although I appreciate the questions raised in these articles, they do little to further the understanding of diet and health so urgently needed today. They also create a false impression about the way macrobiotics is being practiced throughout the world, and add to the public's confusion about what to eat. The following points are especially worth noting.

1. Articles such as these often focus on several isolated cases from the 1960s, in which problems arose due to a misinterpretation of macrobiotic principles. People who have seen their health improve through macrobiotics are rarely interviewed about their experiences; their stories usually never appear in these negative articles.

2. These articles ignore favorable research on the macrobiotic diet. For example, in research conducted by Harvard Medical School, people who eat macrobiotically were found to have lower than average levels of blood pressure and cholesterol, two of the leading risk factors for heart disease.

3. The authors of these articles make the mistake of assuming that people who follow a macrobiotic lifestyle are observing highly restrictive diets, with the goal being to eat nothing but brown rice. That assumption is false. A review of macrobiotic literature shows that current macrobiotic recommendations suggest a broad, flexible diet that includes a wide variety of foods, not a restricted regimen. Writers who attack macrobiotics as an "all brown rice diet" are either biased or have not done enough research. Perhaps they are more interested in sensationalism than in accuracy.

4. These authors fail to note the similarities between macrobiotic dietary guidelines and recommendations advocated by leading health organizations. Macrobiotic guidelines are in similar to the suggestions in *Dietary Goals for the United States* and other official publications. Doctors, nutritionists, and public health authorities around the world agree that a diet based on whole grains, beans, fresh local vegetables, and other foods high in complex carbohydrates and fiber, and low in cholesterol and fat is not only nutritionally adequate, but may be the most effective way to lower the risk of cancer, heart disease, and other chronic illnesses. Moreover, these authors rarely give credit to macrobiotic educators for contributing to nutritional awareness in this country and abroad.

5. These authors overlook the fact that many doctors and health professionals are practicing macrobiotics. Michio Kushi and other macrobiotic educators give regular seminars for doctors and other health professionals. Many doctors now recommend macrobiotics as a viable approach to health promotion and disease prevention.

Because of the increase in chronic illness arising from modern dietary habits, it urgent that the general public be presented with clear, accurate, and current information about macrobiotics. I encourage anyone writing an article about macrobiotics to contact one of the hundreds of macrobiotic educational centers in North America in order to receive up-to-date information or meet with any number of people—including families with children—who are enjoying good health as the result of adopting a macrobiotic diet. I also encourage all of you who are practicing macrobiotics to write your personal story or case history, and to send it to a macrobiotic center for publication. It isn't necessary to have a story about the recovery from cancer or another dramatic illness; cases showing general improvement in physical, mental, and spiritual health are just as important.

Individual efforts do make a difference. For example, once when I was in Washington, D. C. for lectures, I was introduced to a woman from the U.S. Department of Agriculture. She was compiling a textbook on nutrition that was going to be used by millions of high school students throughout the country. She had heard that I was a macrobiotic teacher, and wanted to show me a draft of the statement describing the macrobiotic diet that was scheduled to appear in the book. Because of her pleasant, upbeat manner, I expected the statement to be positive, or at least accurate. However, I was quite surprised to read what amounted to a denunciation of the "Zen" macrobiotic diet, followed by a warning to young people to avoid it at all costs. The diet described in the statement had little to do with the way people in America were actually practicing macrobiotics, or with the way that macrobiotics was presented in lectures and publications. I told her that the statement was completely inaccurate, and if published, would create confusion and misunderstanding.

Fortunately, she was not biased personally against macrobiotics. She became apologetic once I explained the situation to her. She said a committee was meeting in several days to finalize the book prior to publication and she would be happy to present a statement from me explaining macrobiotics with a recommendation that it be used in place of the earlier one. I sat down with a pen and paper and quickly drafted a letter explaining the situation. I added a brief statement about the macrobiotic diet, and gave both of these handwritten documents to her. She thanked me and said she would let me know about the outcome of the meeting. As it turned out, the committee decided to omit the section on macrobiotics once they realized the information they had was inaccurate.

Together we can change the misconceptions and unnecessary confusion that surround the practice of macrobiotics. Let us encourage people everywhere to adopt this simple, common sense approach to to health and peace. Let us offer macrobiotics as a solution to the modern crisis and a way to transform the earth into paradise.

Source: This essay is based on a letter in *Order of the Universe*, Boston, Mass., 1977.

6. Suggestions for United States Food Policy

In the summer of 1977, Michio Kushi asked me to draft a memorandum with suggestions for the national food policy recommendations he was preparing for the Carter Administration. President Carter had ordered a reassessment of United States food policy following the release of *Dietary Goals for the United States* earlier that year. Through my office at the East West Foundation, arrangements were made for Michio to meet with members of Carter's domestic policy staff at the White House. The meeting took place in September.

In the memorandum, I recommended that the federal government pursue active programs in the following areas.

1. Organic farming and traditional food processing. I suggested that the federal government encourage the large-scale adoption of natural and organic farming methods, especially the cultivation of whole grains, beans, and fresh local vegetables for direct human consumption. I also suggested that the government encourage the production (using organic natural methods) and use of traditional soybean foods, such as miso, tamari soy sauce, tofu, and tempeh, as low-cost, high-quality sources of protein. Also included was a suggestion that the government provide guidance and funding to farmers to convert from present chemical-intensive methods of food production to natural and organic methods, and encourage the harvesting and distribution of edible sea vegetables as high-quality sources of minerals.

2. Distribution of high-quality natural foods. I recommended that the federal government encourage the distribution and marketing of high-quality natural foods, while funding research on the costs of converting the present food system toward the goal of making healthful natural foods available to the public. Included in this recommendation was a suggestion that the government fund a program of education on the relationship between diet and health for representatives of the food industry.

3. Research on diet and health. Included in the memorandum was a suggestion that the federal government fund an active program of research on diet and health, including the use of the macrobiotic diet in the prevention and possible recovery from cancer, heart disease, diabetes, and other chronic disorders.

4. Public education. I also recommended that the federal government provide funding for an active campaign to educate the public about the relationship between diet and health, both through the media and through public institutions. The purpose of this campaign would be to provide people with enough information to make food choices consistent with good health, and to present practical guidelines for preparing and using healthful natural foods.

After reviewing these and other suggestions, Michio drafted a series of comprehensive recommendations aimed at improving the health of the American people. This document served as the starting point for the meeting with Carter's advisors. I sent Michio's recommendations to members of the Senate committee that drafted *Dietary Goals*, and to doctors and researchers around the world. (The *Food Policy Recommendations* are in the book, *On the Greater View*, by Michio Kushi, Avery Publishing Group, 1986.) I also included a copy of the East West Foundation's landmark report, *A Nutritional Approach to Cancer.*

Below are several of the replies I received:

Thank you for sharing with me copies of your organization's publications, *A Nutritional Approach to Cancer* and *Food Policy Recommendations for the United States.* I am sure the documents will serve as significant resources in future congressional discussions in these areas. Your comments on the work of the Select Committee are appreciated. I would like to be kept informed of the nutrition and health related concerns of your foundation.

Bob Dole
United States Senate
Subcommittee on Nutrition

Thank you for your letter and the enclosed reports on food policy and the relationship between our diet and our health. I share your concern over this important issue and during future considerations of legislation relating to the importance of nutrition to proper health care in the nation, the reports prepared by the Foundation will continue to be most helpful. Again, I appreciate having the benefit of your views.

> Edward M. Kennedy
> United States Senate
> Committee on Human Resources

As you know from my comments in the Dietary Goals, I am in agreement with many of the policy recommendations you have made. I believe continuing efforts must be made both with the executive branch and the Congress, as well as educational institutions, for example through school lunch programs. It is also essential to educate the professions and the media to provide the public with better choices in relation to diet and to help people better understand what those choices really are.

> Philip R. Lee, M.D.
> Professor of Social Medicine
> University of California

Source: This essay is based on personal notes and an article entitled, *Responses to the Food Policy Recommendations for the United States*, published in *Order of the Universe*, Boston, Mass., 1978.

7. Diet and Disease: An Overview

There is now an increasing volume of evidence linking the way we eat with our physical and mental health, leading to a widespread and growing interest, among both medical professionals and the public at large, in applying diet as a solution to the modern health crisis.

There is no question that our health needs have changed over the last eighty years. At the turn of the century, the most important diseases in the United States were infectious diseases such as influenza, tuberculosis, and pneumonia. Since then, the incidence of infectious disease has declined. However, during this time, the rate of chronic illnesses, such as cancer, heart disease, and diabetes, has risen substantially.

During the twentieth century, a profound change took place in the way people eat, leading many to believe that modern dietary habits are the leading cause of the increase in chronic illness. That was the conclusion of the landmark report issued in 1977 by the Senate Select Committee on Nutrition and Human Needs, entitled *Dietary Goals for the United States*, and of reports issued by public health agencies around the world.

To date, more than a dozen international health organizations have issued reports that implicate the modern diet in the rise of chronic disease. Most of these reports make dietary recommendations aimed at prevention. There are signs that preventive dietary guidelines issued over the last decade are producing positive results. For example, the rate of heart disease in the United States and several other countries has declined somewhat over the past ten years. There is evidence supporting the view that this may be due to health conscious dietary changes.

Although many of us have had direct experience with degenerative illness—either personally or through family members or friends—we tend to think that on the whole, those of us in the affluent nations have the best medical care and the most abundant diet, and are thus healthier than ever before. Consider, however, that of the ten leading causes of death in this country, six—heart disease, cancer, stroke, diabetes, cirrhosis of the liver, and arteriosclerosis—are degenerative diseases. These disorders are directly linked to diet. In 1977, about 75 percent of all deaths in this country were from one of these causes, a clear indication that our population is not as healthy as we would like to believe, despite the increasing deployment of medical technology and the convenience of the modern food system.

It is commonly believed that this degenerative epidemic is due to our lengthened lifespan—that the conquest of infectious diseases and consequent lowering of infant and child mortality, in other words, have actually allowed more people to grow older, and that more old people naturally means more degenerative disease. In fact, an increasing proportion of *younger* persons are suffering from chronic disease. Cancer, for example, is the number one cause of death, excepting accidents, of children under fifteen. According to the Summer 1978 issue of *Working Papers*, "The percentage of people under seventeen years old limited in activity due to chronic ailments nearly doubled from 1968 to 1974." Degenerative disease is not an old people's disease, nor is it a necessary result of gains in child survival rates. It affects all people, at all ages, in virtually all populations.

The Changing Modern Diet

Studies of overall patterns of food consumption during the twentieth century reveal a number of interesting trends: (1) there has been a substantial increase in the intake of saturated fat and cholesterol, due largely to rising meat and poultry consumption; (2) there has been a substantial increase in consumption of refined sugar, resulting largely from the addition of sugar to processed foods and increasing soft drink consumption; (3) there has been a tremendous increase in the consumption of chemicals, additives, and preservatives, and a variety of artificial or highly fabricated foods; and (4) there has been a substantial decrease in the consumption of complex carbohydrate foods such as cereal grains, beans, and fresh local vegetables.

In the early part of this century, Americans derived about 40 percent of their caloric energy from complex carbohydrates—cereal grains, beans, and vegetables. This percentage has declined to less than 20 percent. Whole unrefined grains and grain products are practically nonexistent in the modern diet. At the same time, the consumption of fats and simple sugars has risen so that these items now comprise over 60 percent of the diet.

From 1889 to 1961, the ratio of complex to simple carbohydrate dropped more than three times. In 1976, the average person in the United States ate about 120 pounds of refined sugar, compared to less than 40 pounds per person in 1875; an increase of over 300 percent. A large portion of the sugar consumed in this country is eaten in processed foods and beverages, including soft drinks, canned foods, bread, candy, cake, ice cream, breakfast cereals, and others. Soft drink consumption doubled in the United States between 1960 and 1975; increasing from an average per-person intake of 13.6 gallons to 27.6 gallons. In 1975, the average person drank about 295 12-ounce cans of soda, containing 21.5 pounds of sugar.

In 1976, the average person ate nearly 165 pounds of red meat (pork, beef, mutton, veal). The rising popularity of beef is largely responsible for the overall increase in meat consumption. For example, in 1910, the average person ate about 55 pounds of beef. In 1970, this figure had risen to over 113 pounds.

These changes in diet parallel the rise of chronic illness in this century. The connection between diet and disease becomes even more apparent when we review evidence linking diet and cancer.

Cancer and Diet

Much of the scientific evidence linking cancer and diet has come from two sources: (1) epidemiological studies, such as those of overall cancer incidence and changing dietary patterns in the United States, Japan, and other countries; and (2) animal studies such as those which suggest that a restriction of caloric or protein intake has an inhibiting effect on the development of tumors.

Examples of the epidemiological links between diet and cancer are presented below.

1. The decline in cancer incidence in Holland following World War II food shortages. Between 1942 and 1946, the incidence of cancer in Holland dropped 35 to 60 percent, depending on the region of the country. A Dutch epidemiologist, Dr. F. De Waard, has correlated this decline with the changes in diet that occurred as a result of the German occupation of the country. During the occupation, the Germans took most of the cheese, butter, milk, eggs, and meat in the country, leaving the Dutch to live on home-grown vegetables, bread, whole grain porridge, and other basic staples. With the return to normal conditions after the war, the cancer rate jumped back to its prewar level.

2. Changes in cancer incidence among Japanese migrants to the United States. The rates of colon and breast cancer in Japan have, until now, remained rather low, while the incidence of stomach cancer has been high. The opposite is true in the United States. Within three generations, however, Japanese immigrants in this country shift from the cancer incidence patterns common in Japan to those common in the United States. This shift correlates with a change from the standard Japanese way of eating to the modern American one, with a corresponding increase in the intake of meat, chicken, cheese, and dairy food.

3. The worldwide correlation between meat and fat intake and a high incidence of breast and colon cancer. In countries where the intake of meat and animal fat is high, such as Scotland, Canada, and the United States, the mortality rates from colon and breast cancer are also high. Countries such as Japan and Chile, where meat and fat consumption are low, have correspondingly low incidences of these diseases.

The difference between the high incidence of these illnesses in the United States and their low incidence in Japan is consistent with the differences in fat intake between these two countries, and correlates with the increase in the incidence of colon cancer in Japanese migrants to the United States following their adoption of Western dietary habits.

Evidence from specific population groups in the United States reinforces this connection. Groups such as the Seventh Day Adventists, who generally follow a semi-vegetarian regime with a limited fat and meat intake, have a much lower rate of some forms of cancer, especially breast and colon. These diseases have been found to correlate with a low intake of cereal grains which contain dietary fiber. For example, certain African populations who, like the Japanese, have a low-fat, high-fiber regimen, have been found to have correspondingly low incidences of colon cancer. The same appears true for the Seventh Day Adventists.

4. The correlation between the incidence of breast and colon cancer in the United States and increasing consumption of meat and saturated fat, and the declining consumption of grains. The rising incidence of these illnesses correlates with significant changes in the American diet since 1900, especially the rising consumption of meat and saturated fat, and the declining consumption of grains and their products.

5. The increasing incidence of breast and colon cancer in Japan following Westernization of the Japanese diet. The rising consumption of milk and milk products, meat, eggs, oil, and fat that has occurred in Japan since World War II correlates with an increase in the incidences of breast and colon cancer over the past several decades. According to the National Cancer Institute, this increase is "consistent with the Westernization of the Japanese diet during recent decades, particularly with an increased intake of fat."

While epidemiological evidence such as this has been accumulating, animal studies have reinforced the link between cancer and diet. Examples quoted below are from the 1977 *Status Report* of the Diet, Nutrition, and Cancer Program of the National Cancer Institute.

1. Studies showing that a restriction of calories inhibits the development of tumors. A number of animal studies have shown that of all dietary modifications tried so far, the restriction of food intake has had the most regular influence on the development of tumors. A restriction in overall caloric intake has been regularly found to inhibit the formation of tumors and increase life expectancy of experimental animals. Similar trials have also shown that among rats fed identical diets, the incidence of tumors is consistently higher in heavier animals.

2. Studies showing a higher incidence of tumors in animals fed high-protein diets. According to the NCI report, a lower protein intake inhibits the development of spontaneous or chemically induced tumors. Comparisons of a 5 percent and a 20 percent casein diet on aflatoxin induced tumors showed rats on the higher protein diet had a 50 percent greater incidence of cancer. All of the high protein rats developed tumors or precan-

43

cerous lesions, while those on the lower protein diet had no tumors or precancerous lesions.

3. Studies showing a relationship between a high-fat diet and a higher incidence of breast and colon cancer. A number of studies have shown that an increase in the amount of fat in animal diets produces an increase in the incidence of certain cancers, and that the cancers tend to develop earlier in the life of the animal. According to the NCI report, "Tannenbaum has shown that an increase from 25 percent to 28 percent fat in the diet of mice results in a double incidence of spontaneous mammary cancers."

4. Studies suggesting that a natural foods diet contains "protective factors" against cancer. In one group of studies mentioned in the NCI report, irradiated mice consuming a natural foods diet had a markedly lower incidence of tumors than similar mice receiving a highly refined diet. According to the report, these studies suggest "the presence of a protective factor in natural food diets."

Cancer Recoveries

Together with scientific evidence such as this, a small but significant number of case histories and personal accounts have been gathered and publicized, pointing to the use of the macrobiotic diet in the prevention and control of cancer and other chronic illnesses. Although much of this evidence is anecdotal, and has come from outside the realm of official research, many of these accounts begin to seem plausible when considered together with mounting scientific evidence linking diet and cancer.

Since 1975, the East West Foundation has compiled and published case histories which show that a balanced macrobiotic diet can aid in the recovery from cancer. These published case histories (such as those in the book *Cancer-Free*, Japan Publications, 1992) represent only a small number of the thousands of similar experiences that have yet to be documented and published.

Toward a Preventive Nutrition

As we saw in our study of changing dietary patterns in the United States, the modern diet has become much more extreme. Overall consumption of humanity's traditional, centrally balanced staples—whole grains, beans, and fresh local vegetables—has declined, while more extreme foods, such as meat and sugar, chicken and tropical fruit, eggs and chocolate, have become the mainstay of the diet. This shift in dietary patterns has had a disastrous effect on human health, and is the underlying cause of the rise of degenerative illness in the twentieth century. Regardless of whether we approach the modern decline in health from the more traditional, macrobiotic perspective, or through modern epidemiological studies, our conclusion is similar. In order to secure health, both individually and as a society, we must return to a more naturally balanced way of eating in harmony with our environment and with our dietary traditions.

Source: This essay is from an article entitled, *Diet and Disease: An Overview*, published in *Cancer and Diet*, East West Foundation, Boston, Mass., 1980.

Living Water

At a lecture at a large natural food supermarket near Detroit, I was surprised to see a large sign proclaiming, "We use only natural purified water in our snack bar." Upon further investigation, I discovered that they were distilling water, adding minerals to it, and using it for cooking and drinking. They were also recommending it to customers.

During the lecture, I questioned the concept of distilled water. Water from the earth is charged with energy. Distilled water is not. Distilling water is like removing the outer coat of brown rice to produce white rice. We are left with a nutritionally deficient product. Adding minerals to distilled water is like "enriching" white bread with the vitamins and minerals removed during the refining process. Distilled water cannot help us establish health, nor can refined foods. Natural spring or well water is recommended for the establishment of health.

8. A Solution to the Global Energy Crisis

Throughout the world, millions of people are becoming interested in the relationship between diet and health. Interest in more naturally balanced diets has become especially widespread during the past decade, and has arisen as a result of a number of factors, including the following.

1. The continuing rise in the incidence of chronic illness, including cancer, cardiovascular disease, arthritis, diabetes, and others.

2. A continual deterioration in the quality of the modern diet that parallels the documented decline in national health.

3. The publication of numerous medical studies that scientifically document the relationship between diet and health, together with reports prepared by leading public health agencies recommending a diet based on whole grains, beans, and fresh local vegetables for the prevention of chronic disease.

4. The rapid growth of the natural food movement.

5. The increasing popularity of macrobiotic educational programs throughout the United States and abroad.

Not surprisingly, these developments are forcing a reevaluation of many previously held concepts in nutrition. Within the nutritional and health professions, a growing number of people are now convinced that the modern high-fat, high-sugar, and highly refined diet is a primary cause of the rise of chronic illness in the twentieth century. These people favor widespread implementation of preventive dietary strategies.

Those who support the concept of preventive nutrition divide foods into two general groups: (1) foods associated with overall health and the freedom from chronic illness; and (2) foods associated with an increased risk of degenerative disease.

Foods in the more beneficial category include whole grains, vegetables, beans, and other complex carbohydrate foods, fruits, and low-fat forms of animal food such as fish. High-risk foods are generally those high in saturated fat, such as meat, milk and other dairy products, and eggs, along with highly refined foods such as sugar, refined salt, and foods containing additives and preservatives.

The macrobiotic diet is based on foods in the first category, and is consistent with the recommendations of leading public health organizations. Moreover, the benefits of macrobiotics extend far beyond personal health. Macrobiotics offers not only an optimum diet for the prevention of illness, but a highly economical approach to the allocation of global energy resources.

For example, the macrobiotic diet encourages the following energy-conserving practices:

1. The direct use of high quality vegetable proteins.
2. The use of whole rather than refined foods.
3. The avoidance of highly processed, chemically produced foods.
4. The use of regionally produced foods.
5. The return to home cooking.

A large-scale shift toward a diet based on whole cereal grains, beans, naturally processed items such as miso, tamari soy sauce, tofu and other traditional soyfoods, locally-grown vegetables, and other regional supplements could result in substantial reductions in our present energy needs. A 15 percent reduction would be roughly equal to the yearly volume of energy now imported from the Middle East. A growing number of people have shifted toward healthful, energy-efficient diets. In North America alone, more than 20,000 retail stores and cooperatives now carry high-quality natural and ecologically produced foods. This shift has developed largely as the result of concern over the relationship between diet and health, and has begun to produce a small but potentially significant impact on the modern agricultural and food system.

If the shift toward healthful ecologically balanced diets continues, a significant portion of the population in the developed nations may be eating a more energy-efficient diet in the near future. Much of the concern over present and future energy shortages is based on the assumption that people are unwilling to make the changes in lifestyle necessary to reduce overall consumption. However, the success of the macrobiotic and natural food movements over the past twenty years proves that people *are* capable of making fundamental changes. The macrobiotic diet offers a solution not only to problems of personal health. By encouraging the more efficient use of energy and natural resources, the macrobiotic lifestyle—if widely implemented—could offer a long-term solution to the global energy crisis.

Source: This essay is taken from the *Introduction* to the *Case History Report*, Volume 7, East West Foundation, Boston, Mass., Summer, 1980; and an article entitled, *World Health, World Peace* in *Cancer and Diet*, East West Foundation, 1980.

Friends of the Earth

In the spring of 1993 I met with the director and staff of Friends of the Earth at their headquarters in Washington, D. C. The purpose of our meeting was to discuss the role of macrobiotics in personal and planetary health. During the discussion, I described several ways that a grain- and vegetable-based diet benefits the environment. One staff member mentioned that changing to a grain-based diet is now the most common environmentally-motivated action taken by FoE members around the world. Like the medical community, the environmental movement is now becoming aware of the importance of a balanced natural diet.

9. Making Peace with the Earth

Thousands of years ago, Hippocrates taught that food was the best medicine. He used term *macrobiotics* to describe a way of eating and living in harmony with nature's laws. A naturally balanced diet is central to the practice of modern macrobiotics, just as it was in the system of healing developed by Hippocrates. Food is the vital link between our bodies and the environment, and the quality of food determines the quality of our life. A balanced diet is the key to personal health and well-being. It is also the key to solving the environmental crisis.

Life was able to develop and flourish on earth because of the delicate balance of yin and yang, or the energies of expansion and contraction, on our planet. The earth's large, but structurally compact form (yang) is counterbalanced by the more diffuse, liquid and gaseous envelope that surrounds it (yin). Plants, which are yin, maintain the dynamic balance of the atmosphere. They absorb and utilize more yang carbon dioxide and expel yin oxygen. The oxygen they provide is essential to human and animal life. Animals, which are yang, interact with the atmosphere in the opposite way. They absorb yin oxygen and discharge yang carbon dioxide. Together, plants and animals create a beautiful harmony that sustains life on earth.

Modern civilization is disrupting the natural balance of yin and yang that has existed on the planet for millions of years. On the whole, civilization has become increasingly yang: the speed of change is accelerating daily and we are using more and more intense forms of energy. Rather than slowing down, we can expect this trend to accelerate in the near future.

Because of these activities, the atmosphere is changing. Since 1958, atmospheric concentrations of carbon dioxide have increased by 25 percent, mostly as the result of burning oil and coal. The United States and the former Soviet Union account for about 45 percent of worldwide emissions of carbon dioxide. Meanwhile, we are systematically destroying tropical rain forests that absorb carbon dioxide.

Global Warming

Increases in carbon dioxide and other gases produced by industry, agriculture, and the modern food system are causing the atmosphere to become yang—dense, thick, and heavy. Ideally, the atmosphere should be light and clear (yin), in order to balance the compact structure of the earth and support life. According to environmental scientists, these changes could lead to problems on a global scale. Proponents of global warming believe that some of the reflected heat produced by sunlight no longer radiates back into space. According to this theory, the atmosphere, which has become more yang, causes heat radiation (also yang) to be deflected back to earth, creating what is known as the greenhouse effect.

A growing number of people believe that the greenhouse effect is causing average temperatures on earth to rise, a phenomenon known as global warming. As a result, the polar ice caps could melt, resulting in worldwide flooding, and climatic patterns that have existed for centuries could change drastically. Modern technology has disrupted the natural cycle of carbon in the atmosphere, with potentially far-reaching consequences. Disruption of the carbon cycle by modern technology parallels the inefficient use of organic carbon compounds—or carbohydrates—in the food chain. Before the industrial revolution, the majority of people ate carbohydrates in their most efficient form. Traditional diets were based on whole grains, beans, fresh local vegetables, and other complex carbohydrate foods.

The modern food system no longer relies on these energy-efficient foods. It is based instead on the highly inefficient conversion of complex carbohydrates, often in the form of grains and beans, into animal protein and fat. Feeding these valuable foodstuffs to livestock and then eating them in the form of animal food wastes a tremendous amount of raw materials and energy. One expert estimated that if the world were to adopt this method of food production, all of the known reserves of petroleum would be exhausted in thirteen years.

Modern food production contributes a great deal of carbon dioxide and other greenhouse gases to the atmosphere. Cattle ranching, for example, is the single largest source of methane, a leading greenhouse gas. Whole grains, beans, and vegetables are far more energy-efficient than animal products. Corn or wheat return 22 times more protein per calorie of fossil fuel expended than does beef produced on the modern feedlot. Soybeans are 40 times more energy efficient than modern beef.

In *Diet for a New America*, John Robbins describes the energy savings that would result from a shift toward whole grains, beans, and vegetables. He cites a report by economists Fields and Hur:

> A nationwide switch to a diet emphasizing whole grains, fresh fruits and vegetables—plus limits on export of nonessential fatty foods—would save enough money to cut our imported oil requirements by over 60 percent. And, the supply of renewable energy, such as wood and hydroelectric, would increase 120 to 150 percent.

In order to slow the expected rate of global warming predicted to occur because of the greenhouse effect, scientists estimate that fossil fuel emissions would have to be cut by about 60 percent. Unfortunately, however, as the modern diet and way of life spread around the globe, economists predict that these emissions will actually *double* over the next forty years.

Destruction of forests, including tropical rain forests, can also be traced to the modern diet. Forests are being cut to make room for grazing livestock or for growing livestock feed. According to one estimate, if deforestation continues at the present rate, there will be no forests left in the United States by 2040. Moreover, countries in Central and South America are systematically destroying tropical rain forests that contain up to 80 percent of the world's land vegetation and provide a substantial amount of the planet's oxygen.

The refining, processing, refrigeration, and other techniques used in the modern food system waste a tremendous amount of energy and contribute to global pollution. Sugar refining, for example, is a highly mechanized process that utilizes fossil fuels, as does the production of the chemical fertilizers and pesticides used in modern agriculture. Nitrous oxide, another greenhouse gas, is largely a product of chemical fertilizers.

In the human body, the intake of animal foods causes saturated fat and cholesterol to build up in the blood and eventually clog the arteries and blood vessels. If this process continues

51

unchecked, it can lead to collapse of the body due to heart attack or stroke, or to accumulation of fats and toxic substances in the organs leading to cancer. A similar situation is developing in our environment, due to the inefficient use of carbohydrates in the form of animal protein and fat. Pollution caused by industry and the modern food system is contributing to the accumulation of carbon dioxide, methane, nitrous oxide, sulfur dioxide, and toxic chemicals in the environment. The buildup of these substances threatens the earth's ecosystem with collapse.

Depletion of the Ozone Shield

At the outer reaches of the atmosphere is found a very thin envelope of gas, ozone, that acts as a natural screen for the sun's rays. Solar radiation polarizes into more yin ultraviolet and more yang infrared rays. Ozone is a very yin gas made up of three atoms of oxygen. Because like repels like, it blocks or repels ultraviolet radiation while letting infrared rays pass through. Now, however, because of the modern diet and lifestyle, we are punching holes in the delicate layer of ozone high in the stratosphere. According to *Newsweek*:

The problem is a close as the air conditioner in your window or the fast-food container at your feet. Both can release chlorofluorocarbons (CFCs) into the atmosphere. Once free, these chemicals float toward the heavens. About 15 miles up they encounter the ozone layer, a paper-thin (three millimeter deep) sheet that envelops the planet and shields it from ultraviolet (UV) radiation. Under the right conditions, the CFCs destroy ozone.

Ultraviolet light can weaken or damage the cells of the immune system. Cells that initiate the immune response are more yang and are especially vulnerable. At the same time, UV radiation causes the body to accelerate production of more yin suppressor cells that shut down the body's immune response. Depletion of the ozone layer could lead to an increase in immune deficiency diseases, including leukemia and skin cancer, especially when extreme yin foods and beverages such as sugar, tropical fruits, and oils and fats are weakening the immune response from the inside.

52

When our diet is based on a high intake of animal foods that contain plenty of fat, and when these foods are cooked with modern energy intensive methods, such as grilling, broiling, or deep frying (as they are in fast food restaurants), our body temperature rises and we become less able to tolerate warm weather. This increases our need for air conditioning, and our desire for iced foods and beverages that require constant refrigeration. CFCs are used as coolants in refrigerators.

Diet and the New Ecology

Eating whole grains, beans, fresh local vegetables and other whole natural foods is the first step toward restoring the environment. By eating energy-efficient foods in harmony with climate and season, especially those grown organically, we are supporting a system of farming and food production that will preserve the soil, water, and air for a countless number of future generations.

Our internal and external environments are intimately related. Personal health is equivalent to planetary health. The principles of natural living that underlie the macrobiotic way of life apply as much to healing our planet as they do in restoring our personal health.

Source: This essay is based on an article entitled, *Energy-Efficient Foods: Macrobiotics and the Environment*, published in *One Peaceful World*, Becket, Mass., Spring, 1989.

10. A Letter to Bill Clinton

In August, 1992, Bill Clinton received the Democratic Party's nomination for president. Below is a letter I sent to him in which I outlined the macrobiotic approach to personal and planetary health, together with suggestions for including preventive diet in his national health care plan.

Dear Governor Clinton,

Those of us in the macrobiotic, natural food, environmental, and holistic health movements congratulate you on being selected as the Democratic Party's candidate for president, and on your choice of Albert Gore as your running mate. We appreciate Senator Gore's strong stand on environmental issues and his commitment to a cleaner and healthier planet.

For the past thirty years, my associates and I have been working to promote awareness of an ecologically balanced diet. It is my firm belief that an environmentally sound lifestyle begins with the selection of whole natural foods. Under the name of macrobiotics, millions of people throughout the world have begun to eat a more natural, ecologically balanced diet based on whole cereal grains, fresh local vegetables, and other products of regional, non-polluting, and self-sustaining agriculture.

Evidence is accumulating that a diet based on these foods may be of enormous benefit to personal health. The basic principles of macrobiotics—for example, reducing the intake of high-fat animal food, sugar, and refined foods, and basing the diet on whole grains, beans, and fresh local vegetables—have been endorsed by the United States Senate in the landmark 1977 report, *Dietary Goals for the United States*; by the National Academy of Sciences in the 1982 report, *Diet, Nutrition and Cancer*; by the U.S. Surgeon General in the 1988 report, *Diet and Health*; and by reports issued by other scientific and public health agencies in this country and abroad.

Around the world, a consensus is building that a naturally balanced diet along the lines of macrobiotics would substantially reduce the incidence of chronic disease.

In his 1992 State of the Union address, President Bush announced that medical costs in the United States reached $800 billion in 1991, and will climb to a staggering $1.6 trillion by the year 2000. I firmly believe that the continuing escalation of medical costs will severely disrupt the world economy by the early part of the next century. The economic benefit of reducing the number of chronic diseases in the United States would be tremendous. Given our current situation, the need for preventive health strategies, including proper diet, has never been more urgent.

The rising cost of health care requires bold new initiatives in the realm of disease prevention and health promotion. The federal government can play a vital role in promoting public health and reducing the demand for health care services by:

1. Conducting an active program of public education on the importance of low-cost preventive diets and related health practices.

2. Devoting a larger share of the federal budget to research on diet and health, including the role of a low-cost, natural foods diet in the prevention of cancer, heart disease, and other chronic illnesses.

3. Exploring, through research, the role of a natural foods diet as a low-cost form of adjunctive therapy in the recovery from chronic illness.

These simple proposals offer the promise of improved public health and a steady reduction in health costs. Education on low-cost, preventive diet shifts the focus (and the burden) of health care away from the health care system and to the individual consumer. It empowers the individual and fosters self-responsibility by providing people with the tools they need to stay healthy. At this critical juncture, I feel it is urgent for you to include preventive health care, especially the role of a naturally balanced diet, as a major component of your forthcoming health care plan.

Not only is the modern diet a primary cause of the rising incidence of chronic disease, it is also a major contributor to the continuing degradation of the environment. The modern food system is based on the inefficient conversion of foods such as cereal grains and beans into animal protein and fat, in the form of meat, chicken, milk, cheese, butter, and eggs. This process wastes a tremendous amount of energy, largely in the form of fossil fuels. The burning of fossil fuels by various segments of the food industry contributes a great deal of carbon dioxide to the atmosphere, and is a primary contributor to global warming.

It is far more efficient to eat plant foods directly. Whole grains, beans, fresh local vegetables, sea vegetables and other foods produced by regional organic agriculture are far more energy-efficient than modern beef, chicken, and other forms of animal food.

Destruction of the rain forest is also linked to the modern diet. As you may know, cattle ranching is a leading cause of tropical deforestation. According to Edward O. Wilson, 55,000 square miles of rain forest (an area larger than the state of Florida) disappears every year. The wholesale destruction of this invaluable natural resource would be substantially reduced if America shifted toward a grain- and vegetable-based diet.

I would be happy to discuss these issues in person with you or with Senator Gore. I would be able to meet with you during the campaign if you plan to visit Massachusetts or after the election in Washington. Feel free to contact me at your convenience if you would like to arrange such a meeting. I would like to hear your views and those of Senator Gore about the possibility of focusing public attention on the role of diet in personal and planetary health, and the possibility of reducing medical costs by implementing preventive strategies that incorporate a naturally balanced diet. I wish you success in the coming months, and look forward to hearing from you.

Source: This essay is based on personal correspondence, August and December, 1992.

Part III: Exploring the Order of the Universe

11. Balance in the Art of Cooking

Cooking is the art of creating life itself. From it arises happiness or unhappiness, success or failure, health or sickness. The quality of our diet determines whether our life is one of continuing health and development, or one of progressive decline and decay. Cooking is so vital that every person, both male and female, is encouraged to develop a good working knowledge of how to select and prepare basic daily foods. This education can begin at home as soon as a child is able to understand, and can continue throughout life. Proper cooking is essential to every aspect of our life and destiny, yet we rarely find a school or college that includes basic cooking in its curriculum.

The modern world is facing many difficulties brought on largely as a result of ignoring the importance of food and cooking. One need only refer to the statistics that record the rise of cancer, heart disease, stroke, mental illness, and other chronic disorders, together with social decline and disorder, to confirm just how widespread are the challenges that confront us as individuals and as a society. As large as these problems seem and as illusive as their solutions appear to be, each can be traced back to what takes place in the kitchen. A peaceful and healthy world will not be created at conference tables, in scientific laboratories, in college or university seminars, or through international negotiations or discussions. It will emerge as we come to understand the importance of food and begin to apply that understanding in our daily lives. In a very real sense, a healthy and peaceful world begins in the kitchen.

In the midst of the physical and social decay that confronts us, however, is the growing awareness that proper food and proper cooking is the way to reverse our modern predicament. From the steadily expanding natural foods movement, to the emerging interest among leaders in government and medicine,

59

we see the growth of a realistic attitude toward food and its relationship to our complete well-being.

Macrobiotic Principles

In macrobiotic cooking, we try to make balance with our natural environment. The origin of balance is the two fundamental forces found throughout the universe. In macrobiotics, we refer to these universal forces as yin and yang.

Yin represents the primary expansion of the universe, and produces such tendencies as centrifugality, expansion, low temperature, upward growth or motion, diffusion, lightness, and countless other appearances. Yang represents the primary force of condensation or materialization that arises within the infinite depth of the universe. It produces such relative appearances as centripetal force or movement, contraction, high temperature, downward growth or motion, density, heaviness, and countless other appearances.

In macrobiotic cooking, we apply the various yin and yang factors in our food and environment to create balanced meals. The more yang or contractive environmental factors include fire, pressure, salt, and time (aging); while the more yin or expansive factors are oil, water, lack of pressure, and less cooking time (freshness). Foods, like every phenomena in the universe, can be classified into two general categories, beginning with the distinction between foods that come from the vegetable kingdom (yin), and those from the animal kingdom (yang). Then, within each category of food, individual items can be identified as being either more yin or more yang.

Cooking, for the most part, is the process whereby we take yin, vegetable foods and bring them into the center by making them more yang with fire, pressure, salt, aging, and other factors. In all but the most extreme polar climates, cooked vegetable-quality foods can comprise the mainstay of our diet. Eating a plant-based diet makes balance with our biological needs. Proceeding along the scale from yang to yin, daily foods can be classified as follows: (1) salt, eggs, meat, poultry, and fish, all of which have more extreme contractive energy; (2) whole cereal grains, beans, local vegetables, seeds, nuts, and temperate fruits, which in general have more balanced energies; and (3) tropical fruits, concentrated sweeteners, refined sugar, chemical additives, and drugs and medications, all of which are extremely expansive. Among dairy foods, hard, salty cheeses are extremely yang, while milk, yogurt, cottage cheese, and butter are extremely yin.

In order to create the ideal conditions for health, we need to choose foods that are centrally balanced in terms of yin and yang. Cereal grains are generally the most balanced among daily foods, and it is for this reason that they can comprise the mainstay of our diet, followed by locally grown, seasonal vegetables, beans, and sea vegetables, in addition to such supplementary foods as white meat fish, seasonal fruits, seeds and nuts, condiments and seasonings, and others that are generally within the centrally balanced range.

Through macrobiotics, we can easily maintain physical, mental, and spiritual health. However, health is not the final goal of macrobiotics, but only a means to the enjoyment of life and the realization of our dreams. Simple, natural, whole foods, when properly prepared and aesthetically served, are actually the most appealing to our taste. We should not have the feeling that we are denying ourselves any particular taste or range of foods, but need to understand that through macrobiotics, our appreciation of taste expands tremendously. The goal of macrobiotic cooking is to prepare meals that are healthful, balanced, and thoroughly enjoyable.

Once you are able to use natural and healthful ingredients to create attractive and delicious meals, you begin to understand that you are not following a particular diet but instead are eating in the way a human being was intended to. At the same time, you begin to realize that proper food is the key to a healthy, peaceful, and happy life—the secret that has been in front of us all along.

Source: This essay is from the *Foreword* to *An Introduction to Macrobiotic Cooking*, East West Foundation, Boston, Mass., June, 1978.

12. Albert Einstein and the Order of the Universe

The year 1979 marked the hundredth anniversary of Albert Einstein's birth. Several national magazines commemorated the occasion by publishing summaries of his theories. Within the scientific community, Einstein is generally regarded as the greatest thinker of the modern era. Accordingly, let us review several of his ideas from the perspective of the unifying principle.

1. $E=mc^2$ (energy is equivalent to matter; matter is equal to energy). In macrobiotic thinking, everything is constantly changing. Day becomes night, winter becomes summer, activity becomes rest, energy becomes matter, and matter becomes energy. Einstein's formula is essentially a statement of the law of change.

Einstein's view of the unity of matter and energy is similar to the traditional Oriental concept of Ki. In the view of Oriental philosophy, Ki, or universal energy, assumes an endless variety of forms. It can take more diffuse forms, such as invisible waves, or more dense, solid, and material forms. Energy continually cycles back and forth between yin and yang: invisible waves eventually condense, giving rise to the physical universe; at the same time, all things in the universe eventually decompose and return to the world of energy. In the traditional Far Eastern view, there is no distinct borderline between matter and energy. Both are considered different forms of Ki.

2. Light travels at the constant and unchanging speed of 186,000 miles per second. Macrobiotic cosmology begins from the understanding that *everything changes*. In this universe, the only constant is change itself. It is only in the absolute world, which exists beyond all manifested things, that we find constancy and permanence. Light has both a wave and a particle nature, and exists within the spiral of the relative world. Accordingly, the speed of light must be variable, increasing in proportion to the distance from its source. As light, which is yang, radiates further outward into the darkness of space (yin), its velocity increases, as does the force of attraction which the endlessly expanding depth of the universe exerts on it. Ultimately, it approaches infinite speed, at which time it becomes one with the darkness. At the same time, the darkness of space is continually producing stars, planets, and other infinitesimal points that radiate light. Light changes into darkness and darkness into light in a never-ending cycle.

3. The notion of "curved" space. Einstein's idea that space is curved is similar to the macrobiotic view that all things are created in the form of a spiral. For example, the earth is actually the most dense, visible part of a huge electromagnetic unit that extends into the solar system. This vibrational unit is held in balance by two basic forces: more yang, centripetal energy generated by the universe in toward the planet, and more yin centrifugal force generated outward by the rotation of the earth.

Since the earth is continually rotating, these forces move spirally. Astronomers have detected this pattern in the behavior of small particles above the earth. The sun is continually discharging a stream of energized particles made up largely of ionized hydrogen, or hydrogen that has been broken down into free electrons and protons. These high-energy particles are known as the solar wind, and create a subtle medium that permeates interplanetary space.

When these particles arrive arrive in the vicinity of the earth, they behave in an interesting way. Centrifugal force is strongest at the equator, since that is where the rotation of the earth is fastest. Centripetal force is strongest at the poles. When these particles arrive high above the equator, they are deflected by the strong centrifugal force there and spiral north and south toward the poles. At the poles, they are caught in the strong current of centripetal force and spiral down toward the atmosphere. At the North Pole, they spiral in a counterclockwise direction, the same direction as the earth's rotation. At the South Pole, they spiral clockwise. When these high-energy particles collide with the gases in the upper atmosphere, they produce the phenomenon known as the aurora borealis, or "northern lights."

All celestial bodies, from the sun to planets, stars to comets, galaxies to asteroids, rotate in a spiral pattern. The universe itself is a gigantic rotating spiral. Movement in a straight line is actually an illusion; all motion is spiral motion. It is possible that Einstein had an intuitive awareness of this universal pattern when he suggested that space is curved.

4. The existence of gravity waves. Possibly the most basic concept in modern science is that of universal gravitation, as formulated by Isaac Newton. According to the famous story, Newton conceived his theory after watching an apple fall. He reasoned that the earth was exerting some type of force on the apple that caused it to fall to the ground. Newton extended this concept to include all bodies in the universe, and hypothesized that each exerted an independent gravitational force.

Newton's theory seemed to explain why stars, planets, and the moon are held in their orbits, why the tides ebb and flow the way they do, why water runs downhill, and why things fall to the ground. However, in macrobiotic thinking, Newton's perspective is upside-down. George Ohsawa was the first to examine universal gravitation from a wider view. According to Ohsawa, gravity does not originate within independent physical bodies, such as the earth or sun, but is a unifying property of space itself. Space expands endlessly in all directions. Yet, this expanding force presses in on physical objects from all directions. From our point of view on earth, it appears as an incoming, centripetal force. On the earth, this force pushes everything toward the center of the planet, or down toward the earth's surface. In this view, the earth did not pull the apple down; incoming force from the universe pushed it to the ground.

This incoming force also pushes the planets toward the sun. However, like all other physical bodies, the sun also gives off centrifugal, outward force. This outgoing force holds the incoming force in check and prevents the planets from being instantly pushed into the sun. Instead they revolve around it, although, as Ohsawa pointed out, not in fixed orbits. They gradually spiral toward the sun.

Although Newton explained in general terms the manner in which this force operates, he mistook the result for the cause. From this wider view, we see that his interpretation is not unlike the pre-Copernican notion of the solar system. In this geocentric view, stars, planets, the sun, and other celestial bodies were believed to revolve around the earth. In proposing that gravity takes the form of subtle waves, Einstein was most likely in agreement with Newton's hypothesis about the origin of universal gravitation.

5. The search for a unified field theory. During the Einstein centennial, *Newsweek* published an article, "Of Quarks and Quasars," about Einstein's search for a unified field theory, or one set of laws that govern the whole universe. The article stated:

> For 2,500 years, scientists of the Western world have been on a scavenger hunt, looking for an underlying unity to the universe. They have probed everything from atoms to integers, seeking a single thing or concept that would explain any situation anywhere. Their chief conclusion to date is that this Holy Grail will prove to be not a bit of matter but some primeval force.
>
> Lacking a unified theory the world seems to operate by several sets of rules acting independently of each other: gravity, which rules over the planets and galaxies; the strong nuclear force, governing the mechanics of particles within atomic nuclei; and electromagnetism and the weak nuclear force, which control events as disparate as bolts of lightning and radioactive decay. The task of reconciling them is awesome; Albert Einstein spent thirty years vainly trying to unify only two of the forces, gravity and electromagnetism, and his failure scared off others, who concluded that he must be mired in a scientific backwater. Einstein floundered in a morass of equations. But beyond them, he believed, lay an irreducible simplicity. And it was this aesthetic appeal, more than any pragmatic benefits, that motivated theorists to continue the quest.

So as to help bring this search to a more rapid conclusion, I would like to suggest that a unified theory of life already exists. The Holy Grail that science is searching for may be nothing more than the unifying principle of macrobiotics. The irreducible simplicity that Einstein yearned for can be found in these fundamental laws. Yin and yang explain the universal movement of life; they operate beyond time and space and can be used to explain any situation anywhere.

Why was Einstein unable to see beyond his equations and grasp simplicity of life? For one, he was looking in the wrong direction, analyzing and dividing rather than seeking a broad, unifying synthesis. Although guided by an intuitive awareness of unity, his understanding was conceptual rather than practical. Moreover, the way we interpret the universe is the direct result of the quality of our health, including the functioning of the brain and nervous system. If our physical condition is chaotic and disorderly, our view of life will also be chaotic and disorderly. Rather than appearing as a simple, orderly, and unified whole, the universe appears as a confusing mix of contradictions that are impossible to resolve.

Making Peace with the Universe

Recently, scientists have been promoting the idea of a "violent" universe. In a recent popular science magazine, the subtitle to one article reads: "Red-giants, white dwarfs, black holes and other wondrous things in a universe vaster and more violent than anyone imagined." The image of a violent universe is closely related to the prevalent notion of how the universe came into being: the "big-bang" hypothesis. Why is it that modern scientists see the universe as violent, and imagine it was created in a huge explosion?

The answer can be found in the quality of foods that are consumed widely today.

The modern diet is based on the intake of meat, eggs, poultry, cheese, and other yang extremes. Physically, a diet such as this leads to inflexibility, hardening of the arteries, and the development of deposits of cholesterol and fat throughout the body. Excessive consumption of these foods can lead to heart attack, stroke, various types of cancer, and other degenerative illnesses. Psychologically, a diet high in animal food often results in fear, nightmares, and a tendency toward violence and aggression. It is this physical and mental condition that interprets the universe as violent and envisions creation as a sudden cataclysmic event, something like a sudden heart attack or stroke.

A diet based on these foods limits our scope of vision, so that it becomes hard to conceive of the notion that matter originates from non-matter, or energy. Looking at Einstein's physiognomy, we can see that his early diet included plenty of grains and vegetables, thus he was better able to conceive the fundamental unity of matter and energy. On the other hand, the big-bang hypothesis begins from a more limited, materialistic perspective. It states that the universe began as a primordial lump of matter that exploded, giving rise to stars, planets, galaxies, and all the matter in the universe. However, because it is based on a limited view, it cannot explain where this primordial matter came from. Astronomers have discovered that our universe is expanding; galaxies are flying away from each other at enormous speeds. This expansion is thought to have originated with the big-bang.

If we enlarge our view somewhat, we see that our universe is expanding because the one next to it is contracting. The one next to that is expanding, and so on in an infinite pattern of waves that alternately expand and contract endlessly as part of what Michio Kushi calls the super-universe. The infinite universe, or infinite nothingness, gives rise to polarization, or yin and yang, expansion and contraction, up and down. These primary forces create waves that branch endlessly through time and space. These waves give rise to the super-universe. Within the super-universe, energy condenses into matter, giving rise to a countless number of universes composed of galaxies, stars, and planets. On some of these planets, plant, animal, and ultimately human life arise from this universal movement. The big-bang is simply a product of the modern imagination. Like other incomplete concepts, it will eventually be forgotten and replaced by a new idea.

In order to release ourselves from delusions such as the "big-bang" and the "violent" universe, we need to adopt a less extreme diet based on whole cereal grains, beans, fresh local vegetables, and other traditional foods. A diet of whole grains and vegetables establishes physical health while clearing the mind of delusions. It enables us to unify the worlds of spirit and matter, energy and substance, and see the universe as it is, a peaceful, orderly, and harmonious whole governed by the endless order of change.

Source: This essay is based on an article in the pamphlet, *Science and the Order of the Universe*, Boston, Mass., 1980.

13. Healing the Common Cold

The average person today has several colds a year, an indication that the modern diet and way of life have become increasingly unnatural. Colds are much less frequent among people who eat a naturally balanced diet. Colds represent the discharge of excess from the body that originates in daily diet. The symptoms of a cold are usually nasal discharge—including runny nose—sneezing, coughing, and mild fever. Some people develop pink watery eyes and a slight whitish-yellow eye discharge. Irregular bowel movements and sometimes diarrhea may accompany colds.

Colds primarily involve the upper respiratory organs—the throat, sinuses, and nasal passages. The flu also affects these areas, but usually produces more generalized symptoms. In some cases, it involves the digestive organs, a condition known as "intestinal flu."

When the discharge of a cold involves the upper body—the nasal passages, head, and throat—the primary cause is the overintake of excessively yin items. These can include simple sugars, concentrated sweeteners, fruit and fruit juice, spices, tomatoes, potatoes, and other highly acidic vegetables, soft drinks, ice cream, and too much liquid. When the discharge affects the lungs and middle section of the body, including the stomach, the primary cause is the overintake of these more yin items plus fats and oils, including those in dairy products, poultry, and other animal foods. Discharges that affect the small and large intestines are caused by the overintake of more heavy animal fats in addition to the items mentioned above.

The Cold Cycle

Colds typically follow a natural course. They represent the movement of energy in the body. The typical cold cycle begins with a more yin, expansive and outward phase, and finishes with a more yang, inward, or consolidating phase. The more yin phase is commonly called the acute or early stage of the cold. It generally lasts for three or four days, during which time excess begins to accumulate and is discharged through the upper respiratory tract. The discharge is at first watery and loose, and inflammation spreads throughout the mucous membranes in the nose and throat. Fever begins during this stage and the person may start to discharge through coughing.

Once the initial stage has been completed, the cold cycle enters a phase of consolidation and resolution. This is commonly known as the late stage of the cold. The thin, watery discharge usually becomes thicker and yellowish in color. Appetite and energy start to return. Swollen, inflamed mucous membranes return to a more contracted, normal state. Coughing usually continues through this stage, and may be worse in the evening during the time when energy in the lungs and large intestines is more active.

Ultimately, more normal discharge processes take over the elimination of remaining excess. Discharge is then accomplished through the kidneys, skin, lungs, and intestines. At this time the cold resolves itself and the person's condition returns to normal.

Natural Care of a Cold

People often want to eat less when they have a cold, especially in the beginning stages. When a cold develops, instead of trying to force yourself to eat, it is better to have a variety of simply prepared dishes available when you feel hungry. Grains may be more appealing when soft-cooked or served in soups. Soft brown rice or millet porridges (served hot) are preferred, as are lightly seasoned brown rice, millet, or barley soups with vegetables. It is better to minimize the intake of baked flour products, as these make the intestines tight, although a slice or two of unyeasted sourdough bread, preferably steamed until soft, or whole grain noodles in broth, may be eaten occasionally. Light miso soup and tamari broth soups may be eaten if desired.

It is better to avoid raw vegetables and oil during the recovery period, as these can make the intestines weaker. Vegetables can be lightly steamed, boiled, cooked nishime style, water sauteed, or served in soups and stews. Sweet tasting vegetables, including squash, cabbage, onions, and carrots are especially recommended.

Beans, soybean products such as tempeh and tofu, and sea vegetables may be eaten daily. Fish is best avoided during recovery, although a small amount of white-meat fish may be eaten if desired, preferably in a soup or stew with plenty of vegetables. Desserts can be made with cooked apples and other seasonal fruits, to which a pinch of sea salt can be added to make them less acidic. A small serving of natural, sugar-free dessert may be eaten during the later stages of the cold. Rice or amazake (rice milk) pudding may be served if desired for a mild sweet taste.

Nuts and nut butters, which can create blockage in the intestines, are best avoided during recovery. It is better to avoid juices, sparkling waters, and other more yin beverages when you have a cold. Bancha twig and roasted barley tea are preferable. Cold or iced beverages are best avoided. Foods and beverages are best served hot, warm, or room temperature. A variety of special dishes and drinks can also be prepared to help ease the discomfort of a cold. Lotus root tea helps ease coughing and nasal discharge, and can be taken daily for several days. Ume-sho-kuzu, a soothing drink made from umeboshi plum, tamari soy sauce, and kuzu helps relieve diarrhea, and eases digestive discomfort and aches and pains. It can also be taken daily for several days. Tea made from grated raw daikon with several drops of tamari soy sauce induces sweating and helps relieve fever. It can also be taken once a day for two or three days. Guidelines for preparing these special drinks are described in Michio Kushi's book, *Holistic Health through Macrobiotics*, published by Japan Publications, 1993.

Source: This essay is based on personal notes and lectures.

14. On Unity and Polarity

What is the origin of polarity? Everyone knows, for example, that men and women are different, but where do these differences originate? Polarity does not originate with yin and yang. It originates from unity, from oneness. Polarity is an expression or manifestation of the oneness of the universe. It is found everywhere and in all things.

Let us take an eraser as an example. An eraser has a front and a back, hard and soft parts, dark and light parts, and a part that is used for erasing the blackboard and a part that is not. The eraser is composed of numerous polarities. Multiple polarities exist within this one object, as they do in all objects.

Moreover, the eraser does not exist by itself. It exists in relation to other things, and to the environment as a whole. If we compare the eraser to other things, we see that these comparisons are based on polarity. For example, the eraser is bigger than some things, smaller than others. It is lighter than some things, heavier than others. The eraser also exists in time; its duration is defined by a beginning and an end. The eraser exists for a longer time than some things, and for a shorter time than others.

The human body is composed of polarities. The unity of the self arises from the harmony of opposites. Our body has a front and a back; the front is generally softer and more expanded, and the back, condensed and harder. We have a left and a right side that work together in a complementary way. The body has a center and a periphery, and parts that are hidden and parts that are revealed. The body also has a top and a bottom, or an upper region and a lower one. When taken together, these numerous complementary opposites comprise the unity of our our existence.

If we compare ourselves to other people, we discover that our differences are based on polarity. If we compare men and women, we see that men are larger, and women smaller. Men have less hair on their heads, while women have more. Men have rougher skin and more facial and body hair, while women have less body hair and softer, smoother skin. Their body structures are also different. The female body is softer, more rounded, while the male form is leaner and more compact. Men have more bone and muscle, and women, more soft fat.

A man's thinking tends to be centered more in the left-brain, the source of analytical and rational abilities. A woman's thinking is centered more in the right-brain, where creative, intuitive, and artistic abilities originate. Men have the tendency to formulate a dream or vision and then act in order to realize it. Women tend to go in the opposite direction; they are well-grounded in practical reality and from there, aspire toward an idealistic dream. We can say that women begin from the earth and aspire toward heaven, and men begin from heaven and seek to achieve their dream on earth. In this way, men and women complement each other very well.

Energy from the universe, is constantly coming in to the planet. This energy, which we refer to as heaven's force, moves downward and inward, and is more yang. Meanwhile, the earth is continually rotating and giving off centrifugal force. Earth's force moves upward and outward, and is more yin. Some things are more representative of heaven, while other are more representative of the earth. Men receive more of heaven's force, and women more of earth's force. This fundamental difference in energy is reflected in their body structures and in the way they think.

Although heaven and earth are strongly polarized, they originate in one infinite universe. Because of this, opposites have the tendency to attract, go toward, and seek to be together with each other. That movement occurs throughout the universe, and among men and women, creates the desire to be together physically, mentally, spiritually—on all levels. Unity creates polarity, and all polarized things seek to reunite. Love is a cosmic process—a universal dance, a cosmic drama—that we see acted out again and again in countless forms among countless numbers of people.

Source: This essay is from a lecture at the Macrobiotic Summer Conference, Amherst, Mass., August, 1990.

15. Nine Star Ki and the 1992 Election

According to the Nine Star Ki, 1992 was an 8 Soil year. In ancient numerology, 8 is the number of revolution or change. Indeed, change was the principal theme of the 1992 presidential election. The 1992 election, which many consider a watershed in American politics, represents a generational shift in power, in which the generation that came of age after the Second World War assumed national leadership. The events leading up to this historic change offer a clear example of the hidden influence of Nine Star Ki on world events.

Every year, beginning on February 4th, the earth's atmosphere assumes a certain quality of energy. In some years it is active and moving, in others, subdued and quiet. Ancient philosophers classified these energies into nine types that correspond to the cosmology of the five transformations. The five transformations consist of: upward, expanding energy (tree); very active, diffusing energy (fire); downward, stabilizing energy (soil); very condensed, inward energy (metal); and subtly moving, floating energy (water).

The nine energy types represent variations of these five stages and come around in a repeating cycle of nine years. Each year corresponds to one of the nine stages, and each stage is assigned a number from 9 to 1. The numbers 3 and 4 correspond to upward, tree energy; the number 9 to actively expanding fire energy; the numbers 2, 5, and 8 to downward or soil energy; the numbers 6 and 7 to condensed metal energy; and the number 1 to floating, or water energy. The Nine Ki numbers move downward from 9 to 1, after which the cycle repeats.

Each year has a different energy character, and people born during a particular year tend to personify that character. People born during soil years tend to be more thoughtful and stable, with a somewhat reserved manner of expressing themselves.

People born in tree years tend to be idealistic, romantic, and artistic, often expressing themselves in a bold, dramatic fashion.

The nine star types are discussed in Michio Kushi's book, *Nine Star Ki*, published by One Peaceful World Press. The book includes a chart showing the Nine Ki correspondences to years in the twentieth century, and readers who are interested can refer to this chart to determine which star type they are. Nine Star Ki can shed light on the relationship between the presidential candidates, and explain why Bill Clinton triumphed over George Bush and Ross Perot in the 1992 election.

The Candidates' Nine Ki Characters

George Bush was born in 1924, a 4 Tree year. Bill Clinton was born in 1946, a 9 Fire year, while Ross Perot was born in 1930, a 7 Metal year. Four Trees tend to be romantic and idealistic, and normally have a mature and eloquent way of expressing themselves, except when under pressure, such as in the heat of a presidential campaign, when they sometimes appear superficial. They are attracted to administrative positions, but often are not adept at the day to day details involved in management. This may explain the lack of focus in Bush's 1992 campaign.

Like other 9 Fires, Bill Clinton is an active, passionate type, very good at generating enthusiasm and communicating and dealing with the public. Clinton established a personal connection with many voters during the campaign, and created new styles of communicating during a presidential race by touring the country by bus and appearing on MTV. Clinton's fire nature infused his campaign with energy, enthusiasm, and constant motion.

According to the movement of the five transformations, tree energy supports or nourishes fire energy. Because of his 4 Tree nature, George Bush's natural tendency is to support Bill Clinton's 9 Fire energy. This may help explain why Bush seemed to hold back during the campaign, as if he lacked enthusiasm for the presidential race. He waited until after the Republican convention in August to attack Clinton, and this helped the Democrat maintain his lead in the polls. In one interview, Bush said he respected Clinton personally, and it was only because of the campaign that he was forced to go on the attack.

In contrast to the relationship between Bush and Clinton, the relationship between Bush and Perot was genuinely antagonistic. Perot is a 7 Metal, and according to the five transformations, metal is antagonistic to tree, with the tendency to offset, override, or cancel out the movement of tree energy. Seven Metal people are down-to-earth and practical, in contrast to more idealistic 4 Trees and passionate 9 Fires. During the campaign, Perot gained notice for his direct, matter-of-fact way of expressing himself and for his practical, no-nonsense approach to solving the U.S. deficit.

The antagonism between Perot's metal nature and Bush's tree energy became evident early in the campaign when the two candidates spent a great deal of time attacking each other. These exchanges were especially damaging to Bush, while Clinton remained comfortably on the sidelines. The energy of 9 Fire overrides metal, so Clinton was largely immune from attacks by Perot. In the end, Perot's candidacy benefitted Clinton by drawing many conservative voters away from Bush.

The Candidates' Positions in the Nine Ki Table

The dramatic shift in George Bush's political fortunes over the past year offers an example of the power of Nine Ki cycles. In 1991, following the Gulf War, Bush enjoyed tremendous popularity. His approval ratings among the American public were close to 90 percent. However, one year later, his approval ratings plummeted to near 30 percent, and he lost the support of many voters. In 1991, it seemed assured that he would win a second term as president; yet in 1992, the situation changed into its opposite: his public support eroded and his campaign stalled. Why did this happen?

Each year the nine numbers take different positions relative to each other. They can be arranged in a square or circle with nine sections corresponding to the eight cardinal directions plus the center. Every year, a different number occupies the center, and the energy of that number creates the energy that characterizes that year. The other eight numbers move into different positions around that central number, with each position having a certain nature or character. The year 1991 was a 9 Fire year; meaning that the number 9 occupied the central position; 1992 was an 8 Soil year, with the number 8 in the center; 1993 is a 7 Metal year, and 1994 will be a 6 Metal year. (The numbers move downward from 9 to 1 as stated above.)

The baseline arrangement of numbers occurs whenever the number 5, which corresponds to soil, moves into the center. This arrangement occurs every nine years (1995 will be the next 5 Soil year) and is known as the standard table. During these times, each number and energy is in its "home" position. The standard table is shown in figure 1; please note that in this arrangement, the direction North is shown at the bottom of the chart, while the direction South is shown at the top. Each of the positions on the standard table carries the energy of its home number, so that the position South carries the energy of 9 Fire; North, the energy of 1 Water; East, the energy of 3 Tree; West, the energy of 7 Metal; and so on as we see in the table.

Figure 1—Standard Nine Ki Table

S

	4	9	2	
E	3	5	7	W
	8	1	6	

N

Each year, the numbers move through the different positions on the table. For example, in 1991, Bill Clinton's number, 9 Fire, was in the center (the home position of 5 Soil); in 1992, it moved to the Northwest (the position of 6 Metal); in 1993, it will transit through the West (the position of 7 Metal); in 1994, the Northeast (the position of 8 Soil); and in 1995, the South (its home position on the standard table). In 1996, 9 Fire will transit through the North, the home position of 1 Water.

Our personal destiny is greatly influenced by the quality of energy of each of these positions. When our number moves to the East or South, for example, our destiny is generally positive, bright, and active. It is easier to accomplish our goals. When our number moves to the West, our destiny is generally bright, but our focus is usually more inwardly directed. When our number moves to the North, we enter a period of darkness and stagnation that is not favorable for outward, social progress, although it can be good for self-reflection, learning, and inner development. The character of each of these positions and their influence on personal destiny is presented in Michio Kushi's book, *Nine Star Ki*. Please consult this book for information about your personal destiny from year to year. Now let us look at the way that the movement of numbers affected the outcome of the 1992 election.

Figure 2—Ki Maps for 1991 and 1992

8	4	6
7	9	2
3	5	1

1991

7	3	5
6	8	1
2	4	9

1992

1991 was a 9 Fire year. The energy that year reflected the active and intense character of fire. As we can see in figure 2, George Bush (a 4 Tree) was in the South. The South is the home position of 9 Fire. It corresponds to the energy of summer and midday, and is generally a position of bright, active energy. 1991 was the year of the Gulf War and the collapse of the Soviet Union, and Mr. Bush's position in the Nine Ki table enabled him to achieve broad popular support, so much so that many leading Democrats, including Mario Cuomo, the governor of New York, hesitated to enter the presidential race. This left Bill Clinton, a 9 Fire, in the central position within the Democratic Party.

In 1992, President Bush moved from the South, a highly favorable position in the Nine Ki table, to a highly unfavorable position in the North, the home position of 1 Water. The North corresponds to the energy of deep winter and midnight, and is a time of inactivity, stagnation, and dormancy. Michio Kushi refers to this position as one of darkness, in which one's energy tends to float between heaven and earth. It is a good time for inward spiritual growth, but not good for outward social progress. In short, being in such a low energy position was not advantageous for conducting a presidential campaign.

Throughout 1992, Bush's popularity plummeted, his campaign never hit stride, and he was plagued by poor economic news and Perot's pointed 7 Metal attacks. Moreover, the collapse of the Cold War deprived the Republicans of one of their strongest campaign themes. When coupled with the desire for change that characterizes an 8 Soil year, Bush's position in the North caused him to lose the presidency. Interestingly, toward the end of the campaign, Bush was quoted as saying that 1992 was one of the worst years of his life.

In 1992, Bill Clinton (a 9 Fire) occupied the Northwest, the home position of 6 Metal. This position corresponds to evening and autumn. In the I Ching, 6 Metal represents the energy of heaven, and within the family, the masculine energy of the father. It is a position of power and authority, and as Clinton's success illustrates, a good base from which to conduct a presidential campaign. In short, according to the Nine Star Ki, 1992 was a year of good fortune for Bill Clinton and a year of misfortune for George Bush.

Source: This essay is from an article entitled, *Nine Star Ki and Election 1992*, published in *One Peaceful World*, Becket, Mass., Winter, 1993.

Revolution and the Ki Flow

The breakup of the old Soviet Empire is occurring within an 81-year cycle governed by the energy of 9 Fire. This yin, centrifugal spiral is opposite to the yang, contracting spiral that led to the establishment of a centralized Soviet system in 1917. The new Russian Revolution took place in 1991, a 9 Fire year during which centrifugal force has been especially strong. The month of August, in which these events took place, was an 8 Soil month. The number 8 represents the energy of change, so it was predictable that these developments would occur during this time.

One Peaceful World Newsletter, *Autumn, 1991*

16. Discovering Yin and Yang

Not long ago I received a letter from a student with questions about the discovery method of teaching that we use at the Kushi Institute. The following article is based on my reply.

Thank you for your questions about our way of teaching macrobiotic philosophy at the Kushi Institute. The discovery method has many advantages over other methods of teaching, especially those in which the teacher simply presents information. In regard to the Order of the Universe, which is the class I teach, these advantages can be summarized as follows:

1. The discovery method is a dynamic process that offers both teacher and student the opportunity to explore the varied applications of the order of the universe together.
2. The discovery method addresses students' questions and concerns as the class progresses, while sharpening their ability to think and answer questions.
3. The discovery method allows students to see and experience the order of the universe through practical, common examples, such as the observation of common objects and daily life, and allows students to express their discoveries in class.
4. The discovery method allows students to discover the order of the universe on their own, thus revealing their original, native understanding.
5. The discovery method avoids the static memorization of concepts and information, instead focusing on the development of each student's native intuition.

In the classes on the Order of the Universe, we begin our discovery by seeing how all things are composed of complementary opposites. One way to do this is to invite a volunteer to come to the front of the class and ask the students to make a list of the complementary/opposites that comprise a human being.

We do the same for the complementary factors in the room, and also study different types of movement, seeing how complementary/opposites exist in motion and structure. Through these exercises, we begin to see that complementary/opposites exist everywhere.

Next, we try to make order out of these pairs of opposites by arranging them in a comprehensive classification, with our goal being to see them as a reflection of the most basic forces of nature. In so doing, we discover yin and yang on our own, rather than simply accepting a list or classification compiled by someone else. At this point in the class, our discussions often become dynamic and exciting, with students offering many opinions and asking many questions.

Let me briefly explain how this process works. Before we can develop a consistent yin and yang classification, we need to establish a uniform frame of reference. Using the earth as our common point of reference, it is possible to classify numerous polarities in two columns. For example, if we begin with the polarity between up and down and horizontal and vertical, we see that movement in an upward direction means movement away from the earth, while downward movement implies movement toward the center of the earth. Things with vertical forms have a greater portion of their mass extending upward away from the earth, while things with horizontal forms have a greater portion of their mass lying closer to the earth. Therefore, upward movement gives rise to vertical forms, while downward movement creates horizontal forms.

If we view the earth from a distance, we see that its center corresponds to the inside, while its surface corresponds to the outside. When things fall downward they are actually moving inward toward the center of the earth, while things that go up are moving away from the center and toward the periphery . Based on these consistencies, we can link these pairs of opposites as follows: (1) upward movement, vertical forms, outward movement, and a peripheral (outside) position; and (2) downward movement, horizontal forms, inward movement, and a central (inside) position.

Continuing with this process, we can see that when things expand, they increase in size, and when they contract, the become smaller. Largeness is produced by expansion, and smallness by contraction. These attributes can be related to the above as follows: expanding force makes things gather toward the center, and motion in an upward direction is actually outward, expanding motion away from the earth. Movement in a downward direction is actually a form a contracting motion toward the center of the earth. Largeness and expansion therefore match the characteristics listed as (1) above, while smallness and contraction match those listed as (2).

Once expansion and contraction are added to the list, it becomes relatively easy to classify a variety of other complementary attributes into either of these categories. For example, as things expand, they become lighter and less dense, and become increasingly dense and heavy as they contract. Lightness can thus be classified with the first group of attributes, while density and heaviness can be listed with the second group. Liquids and gases are lighter and more diffuse than solids, and thus go with the attributes listed in the first group, while solid matter is more consistent with the attributes in the second.

In our classes, we categorize a wide range of polarities in this manner. All complementary tendencies display either a stronger tendency toward expansive force or movement, or toward contractive force or movement. These primary forces were given different names by people in various cultures around the world. The ancient Chinese referred to them as yin and yang, and these are the terms we use today in macrobiotic philosophy.

At this critical time in history, it is essential that we understand the principles of macrobiotics and apply them correctly on a daily basis. Macrobiotic principles are the key not only to personal health, but to turning the modern crisis toward health and peace. The discovery method offers an opportunity for everyone to proceed step-by-step toward a genuine understanding of these fundamental principles of life and health.

Source: This essay is from personal notes and correspondence.

17. The Pulse of Life

The rhythm of the heart is symbolic of the pulse of life. The heart is constantly in motion, expanding and contracting without pause. It reflects the alternating rhythm of yin and yang found throughout nature. The heartbeat is produced by the interplay between the forces of heaven and earth. We are constantly receiving energy from the universe. It spirals in from infinite space toward the center of the earth. Heaven's energy moves downward and causes the heart to contract. Meanwhile, the earth is continually rotating. It gives off centrifugal force that moves upward. Earth's rising power causes the heart to expand. As long as these forces are maintained in balance, the heart beats smoothly and without interference.

The human heart is about the size of the fist; in an adult it averages 12 cm in length, 9 cm in width, and 6 cm in thickness. It is enclosed in a double-walled sack called the pericardium. This sack contains fluid that enables the heart to move actively. The heart itself is composed of three layers: a yin, outer layer called the epicardium; a middle layer known as the myocardium; and a yang, inner layer called the endocardium.

The condition of these three layers can be seen in the lines on the hand. The inner, lower line on the hand, sometimes referred to as the "life line," shows the endocardium. The middle line shows the myocardium, and the upper line, sometimes called the "line of intellect," shows the condition of the epicardium. If these lines are deep and clear, it shows that these sections of the heart are strong and healthy. If a line is broken or obscure, it shows potential weakness in the corresponding section of the heart. These imbalances are caused by extremes in diet and way of life.

Similarly, the three sections of the heart can be seen in the three ridges of the ear. The inner ridge shows the innermost region of the heart; the middle ridge, the middle region; and the outermost ridge, the outer region. When the outer ridge of the ear becomes red, it shows that the heart is overactive, due to too many strong yin foods or drinks, including sugar, coffee, fruits, spices, and alcohol.

The Spiral of Circulation

At the center of the circulatory spiral is the heart. The upper orbits of the spiral represent the upper regions of the body; the lower orbits, the lower regions. Blood circulates through the body in the following order: (1) it begins in the heart (yang), and then flows to the lungs (2) in the upper body (yin); to the abdomen (3) in the lower body (yang); to the neck and head (4) in the upper body (yin); to the kidneys (5) in the lower body (yang); to the arms and hands (6) in the upper body (yin); and to the legs and feet (7) in the lower body (yang). The spiral of circulation encompasses seven orbits alternating from yang to yin, and is a perfect representation of the order of nature.

Blood circulates in two directions—from the center (yang) to the periphery (yin), and from the periphery (yin) back to the center (yang). Blood flowing outward from the heart and lungs contains oxygen, a more yin element, and blood flowing from the periphery of the body to the center contains carbon dioxide, a more yang compound. In the heart, blood pressure is at its highest (yang), and it becomes progressively lower (yin) as blood flows outward through the body.

Heart Rate

If we study the rate at which the heart beats (detected by the pulse), we can discover the way in which the forces of heaven and earth, or yang and yin, influence our life. Our heart rate varies according to age and sex as follows (the numbers show the average number of beats per minute):

Age
birth: 140
1 year: 120
10 years: 90
adult: 70

Sex
women: 72-80
men: 64-72

Our heart rate increases with age; also, women have a faster rate than men. Why is this so? Heart rate is generated primarily by the more yin, expanding energy of the earth. Although they are physically yang—small and compact—babies and children are actively growing, which means they are strongly charged with earth's expanding force. As we mature, heaven's energy becomes stronger in our bodies and our heart rate decreases. Women are more strongly charged with earth's force, and thus have a more rapid pulse.

When we stand up, the charge of earth's force in our bodies becomes stronger, and thus our heart rate increases. When we lie down, the charge of heaven's force is stronger, and our pulse and other life functions slow down. Activity means that our bodies are charging earth's energy more strongly; inactivity means that heaven's force has become stronger; thus, heart rate increases with exercise and activity, and slows during rest. Mountains are strongly charged with earth's rising power; valleys with heaven's descending energy. Thus our pulse rate increases at higher altitudes. Emotional excitement is produced by a strong charge of earth's activating force, and thus increases the heartbeat. Oxygen (more yin) is strongly charged with earth's force; it increases the heart rate. Carbon dioxide (more yang) is more strongly charged with heaven's force and slows it down.

Blood Pressure

Blood pressure is the opposite of the heart rate. It increases as heaven's contracting force becomes stronger. It is highest during the contraction of the ventricles, which are the lower chambers of the heart. If we study a picture of the heart, we can see how the lower chambers (ventricles) are more contracted, and the upper chambers (atria) are more expanded. The atria are more strongly charged with earth's force, and thus receive blood from the lungs and other parts of the body. The ventricles are more strongly charged with heaven's force. Thus they contract strongly and propel blood throughout the body.

Blood pressure is expressed as a fraction, for example, 120 over 80. The upper number shows the pressure during the contraction (systole) of the heart; the lower number during the heart's expanding phase (diastole). The systolic blood pressure tends to change with age as follows:

birth: 40
1 year: 80
12 years: 100
20 years: 120
40 years: 125
65 years: 134
after 65: tends to rise

Women's blood pressures tend to average 8 to 10 points lower than those of men until age sixty; after which the blood pressures of men and women tend to become more equal. These averages confirm that blood pressure is primarily a function of heaven's contracting energy. As we saw above, children are strongly charged by earth's force; adults by heaven's energy. As we mature, heaven's contractive force becomes stronger in the body, and thus our blood pressure tends to rise. The female body is more strongly charged by earth's force, and thus women have lower blood pressures than men. However, as a woman ages, she becomes more yang, and her charge of heaven's force becomes stronger. After age sixty-five, her blood pressure tends to become more like that of a man's.

Maintaining the Pulse of Life

Food is the key to keeping the heartbeat smooth and strong. Foods are also charged by heaven and earth. Foods such as meat, eggs, cheese, chicken, and refined salt are extremely contractive. They are strongly charged by heaven's force. Foods like sugar, fruit, soft drinks, ice cream, chocolate, alcohol, and spices are extremely expansive. They are strongly charged by earth's force. Both extremes interfere with the smooth rhythm of the heart.

Eating a diet rich in animal foods (yang) causes the heart and circulatory vessels to become overly contracted. These foods contain plenty of saturated fat and cholesterol which, when eaten in excess, cause the blood to become too thick. Saturated fat and cholesterol eventually accumulate throughout the circulatory system, resulting in blockages that impede the flow of blood. In many people today, blockage of the circulatory system leads to heart attack or stroke. Because the modern diet is so high in fatty animal foods, heart and circulatory disorders of this type affect millions of people and are the leading cause of death in the modern industrialized nations.

Yin extremes also lead to heart disease. Foods like sugar, tropical fruits, alcohol, coffee, and chocolate cause the heart and circulatory vessels to dilate or expand. If they are consumed with regularity, the heart and blood vessels become weak and fragile. The heart may become enlarged and unable to pump blood efficiently. If the blood vessels become weak enough, they may rupture, leading to hemorrhage. When this occurs in the brain, the result is a stroke. In comparison to the type of stroke caused by a blood clot, this type of stroke, known as cerebral hemorrhage, is more yin.

Foods such as whole cereal grains, beans, fresh local vegetables, sea vegetables are not extreme. They conduct heaven and earth's forces in a more even way and can be considered centrally balanced, both in terms of their energy and their effect on the body. They are also low in fat and contain no cholesterol. Avoiding or minimizing extremes and eating primarily centrally balanced foods is the primary way to avoid heart disease. Changing to a more moderately balanced diet can even reverse blockages in the circulatory system and restore weakened blood vessels to a normally healthy condition. By balancing the expanding and contracting energies in our diet and lifestyle, we make the heart strong and healthy and thus maintain the pulse of life.

Source: This essay is based on an article entitled, *The Pulse of Life*, published in *The Rice Paper*, Columbia, S. C., Autumn, 1992.

18. Using Food in Healing

Daily food has the power to heal or make us sick; to keep us healthy or accelerate our decline. The importance of food in health and healing cannot be overemphasized. However, unlike modern nutrition, in which foods are analyzed according to their biochemical effects, the macrobiotic view is based on an understanding of food as energy. Rather than being analytical and partial, the macrobiotic approach is dynamic and whole.

In macrobiotics, we approach food on two levels. In the first, more fundamental level, we apply the principle of yin and yang to balance our daily diet as a whole. Yin and yang help us understand food in terms of energy. Balancing the expanding and contracting energies in our diet is the basis of health and healing. In the second, or symptomatic level, we use food to offset or balance a particular condition or symptom.

Principles of Energy Balance

The key to health and healing lies in our ability to understand food in terms of yin and yang and energy, and to apply that understanding to the structure and function of the human body. For that purpose, we need to view the body in terms of yin and yang. The inner regions of the body, including the bones, blood, and internal organs, are more yang or contracted, while the peripheral regions, including the skin and hair, are more yin or expanded. The front of the body is generally softer and more expanded (yin), while the back is hard and compact (yang). The upper body is generally more yin, while the lower body has stronger yang energy.

On the whole, the right side of the body is strongly charged with yin, upward energy, while the left side is strongly charged by downward, yang energy. This is reflected in the structure of the large intestine, and also in the function of the brain. The large intestine moves upward on the right side of the body, and downward on the left. The right hemisphere of the brain generates more yin, aesthetic or artistic images, while the left is the source of more yang, analytical and rational abilities. Using these basic classifications, we can begin to make specific correlations between the energy of food and the energy of the body.

Day to day, the atmosphere cycles back and forth between upward and downward, or yin and yang energy. Morning is the time when upward energy prevails. Evening and night are the times when downward energy is strongest. In order to maintain optimal health and well-being, we need to orient our lives in harmony with this cycle. In other words, we need to wake up in the morning and be active during the day, and need to get adequate sleep at night. If we go against the movement of atmospheric energy, for example, by sleeping during the day and being active at night, we risk losing our health.

On the most fundamental level, health and healing operate on the same principle. The organs on the right side of the body, including the liver and gallbladder, are strongly charged by yin, upward energy. Those on the left, including the pancreas and spleen, receive a stronger charge of yang, downward energy. Do foods with more expansive energies benefit the pancreas and spleen, or those with more contractive energies? Similarly, what types of foods benefit the liver and gallbladder? As we can see from the daily cycle, we need to go *with* the movement of energy. Thus, foods that match the energy of a particular organ are the most appropriate.

Symptomatic Healing

Symptomatic healing works in the opposite way. Symptoms can be caused by extremes of either yin or yang. In order to neutralize or offset a particular symptom, we use foods that have the a quality of energy that is opposite to that of the symptom. If the symptom is caused by too much yang, we supply the body with yin. When a symptom is caused by excess yin, we need to supply yang.

Constipation offers an example of this principle. Constipation can result from either an excess of yin or yang in the diet. Yang constipation is caused by the overintake of meat, cheese, eggs, chicken, and other forms of animal food, and an insufficient intake of grains, vegetables, and other plant foods containing fiber. It occurs when the intestines become overly tight and contracted. To relieve that symptom, we use foods with an opposite, or more yin energy, such as kanten, lightly steamed greens, grated raw daikon, or vegetables that have been lightly sauteed in oil.

Yin constipation occurs when the intestines become loose, weak, and stagnant because of too much sugar, chocolate, alcohol, spices, ice cream, or soft drinks. To restore the intestines to a more normal, contracted state, a slightly more yang preparation, such as ume-sho-kuzu, would be appropriate.

The Five Energies

As we saw above, the liver and gallbladder are nourished by yin, expanding energy; the pancreas and spleen, by yang, contracting energy. Therefore, according to the principles stated above, if we wish to strengthen the liver and gallbladder, we choose foods that have a slightly more yin, or expansive quality of energy. If we wish to strengthen the pancreas and spleen, foods with slightly more yang energy would be appropriate. Let us see how to apply this principle in the selection of whole grains and beans.

Although whole grains are generally the most balanced among foods, each variety has a slightly different quality of energy. Corn, for example, grows in the summer, and is soft, sweet, and juicy. It has a more yin quality of energy. Buckwheat, on the other hand, grows in cold, northern regions and is very hard and dry. It rapidly absorbs water, and has strong yang energy. Rice has a different quality of energy than barley; millet is different than wheat. Short grain rice is very different than long grain rice. Among the whole grains, therefore, which one is best for the liver and gallbladder, and which one most benefits the pancreas and spleen?

Liver and Gallbladder Traditional philosopher-healers referred to the upward energy that nourishes the liver and gallbladder as *tree* energy. This symbolic name implies growth in an upward direction, as well as movement that branches outward. Among the grains, barley has a light, expansive quality and is classified under the tree energy category. Adding it to brown rice produces a lighter, fluffier, and less glutinous dish. The energy of barley is compatible to that of the liver and gallbladder. Hato mugi, or pearl barley, a species of wild barley originally grown in China, is especially charged with upward energy. Both regular and pearl barley can be eaten several times per week, in soup or with brown rice. Barley tea also supplies the body with light, upward energy and can be used as a regular beverage.

Pancreas, Spleen, and Stomach The spleen and pancreas are charged by an opposite quality of energy that traditional philosopher-healers referred to as *soil* energy. The name soil conveys the image of more compact, downward energy. Millet, a compact grain with a hard outer shell, is a product of soil energy and can be eaten on a regular basis to strengthen the pancreas and spleen. It is helpful in aiding recovery from blood sugar disorders, including diabetes and hypoglycemia. Millet can be cooked with brown rice or used to make delicious millet soup. The stomach is located toward the left side of the body, and is energetically compatible with the pancreas and spleen. Millet is also useful in strengthening the stomach.

Let us now see how the principles of energy balance apply to the selection of whole grains for the other primary organs.

Heart and Small Intestine Compared to the liver and spleen, the heart has a more dynamic, active quality of energy. The heart is located higher in the body (more yin), and is positioned at the heart chakra, a very highly charged region in the center of the chest. Traditional healers referred to this very active stage as *fire* energy. The small intestine is compatible with the heart, and is also charged with active energy. At the center of the small intestine is the highly charged region known as the hara chakra, the primary source of life energy for the entire lower body. Among the grains, corn, a more yin product of summer, is charged with fire energy. It is energetically compatible with the heart and small intestine. It can be eaten fresh in season or used in such traditional dishes as polenta. Whole corn meal or grits can also be used as breakfast cereals.

Lungs and Large Intestine Compared to the heart, the large intestine has more condensed, yang energy. It is located in the lower body, where downward energy is stronger, and although it is large, it is compressed into a small space. The lungs are energetically compatible with the large intestine, and contain many air sacs and blood vessels compressed into a tight space. Traditional healers named this condensed stage *metal* energy. They considered it to be more yang or condensed than the downward, soil energy that charges the pancreas and spleen. Brown rice, especially pressure-cooked short grain rice, has strong condensed energy that corresponds to the metal stage. It can be used as a main daily grain to strengthen and vitalize these organs.

Kidneys and Bladder The kidneys lie in the middle of the body; with one on the right and the other on the left side of the body. Traditional healers felt that the energy that nourishes the kidneys is like water, floating between yin and yang, up and down, although on the whole, downward energy is slightly more predominant. Appropriately enough, they referred to this stage as *water* energy. Beans, which are more yang or contracted than most vegetables, and more yin or expanded than most grains, are a manifestation of floating, or water energy. They strengthen and nourish the kidneys, and their related organ, the bladder. Smaller beans such as azuki and black soybeans have more concentrated energy and are especially beneficial. Beans and bean products can be eaten as a regular part of the diet.

These five stages of energy are actually part of a a continuous cycle. Energy constantly cycles back and forth from yin to yang, moving through the more yin stages tree and fire, and then through the more yang stages soil, metal, and water. This cycle repeats every day and from season to season. Our bodies are comprised of a complex mix of energies that reflect each of these stages, and to maintain optimal health, we need adequate variety in our daily diet.

The five energies can also guide our selection of vegetables and other supplementary foods, as well as our choice of cooking methods. In general, leafy greens are charged with strong upward or actively expanding energy (tree and fire), while round vegetables, such as squash, onions, and cabbage are strongly charged with soil energy. Roots such as carrots, burdock, and daikon have even stronger yang energy (metal), while sea vegetables represent floating or water energy.

In cooking, we change the quality of our foods, by making their energies more yin or more yang. Methods such as quick steaming, blanching (quick boiling), and sauteing accelerate upward (tree) and active (fire) energy, while slow boiling, such as that used in making nishime, condenses the energy in food and corresponds to the soil stage. Pressure cooking is a more yang method of cooking that corresponds to metal energy, while soup corresponds to water energy. Once again, we need a wide variety of vegetables and cooking methods in order to provide the body with a wide range of energies.

Whole grains and other foods in the macrobiotic diet work on both the symptomatic and fundamental levels. On the fundamental level, a food such as hato mugi, or pearl barley, supplies the liver and gallbladder with the upward energy necessary for smooth functioning. At the same time, because of its expansive nature, pearl barley acts symptomatically in dissolving more yang, hardened deposits of animal fat and protein, including cysts and tumors caused by the overconsumption of animal food. Pearl barley tea, for example, is used in Oriental medicine as a beverage to dissolve moles, warts, and other skin growths resulting from excess animal protein.

Food is our best medicine. Balancing the energy of food provides the foundation for achieving good health. Without this foundation, our approach is symptomatic and limited. Understanding food as energy lies at the heart of macrobiotic healing.

Source: This essay appeared in *Macrobiotics Today*, Oroville, Ca, November/December, 1993.

19. Jurassic Science

The image that people have of science is often revealed in popular culture, including art, literature, and film. A variety of recent films offer insight into the way people view the development of science. One of the more popular of these films is *Jurassic Park*. In this film, scientists use genetic engineering to clone dinosaurs. This is done in order to create a theme park, something like Disney World, where people would pay to see real dinosaurs. However, the dinosaurs eventually get out of control, and the people have to run for their lives in order to escape. The implication is that techniques such as cloning and genetic engineering have the potential to cause widespread destruction.

Art is a reflection of life. *Jurassic Park* and films like it reveal an underlying apprehension about recent developments in science. Perhaps they will shock people into thinking seriously about where science is headed. They may also convince people that a change of direction is needed.

There are many examples in history where the techniques of science have been used in an unethical way. The ethics of so-called "double-blind" studies, for example, in which a group of people with a certain illness is given medicine, while a control group is given a placebo, are somewhat questionable. Macrobiotics is difficult to test in this way, because you cannot pretend that brown rice is pizza, or that tofu is fried chicken. Moreover, when someone adopts macrobiotics for a particular illness, that is a fully conscious choice. The decision to change your diet to overcome illness is actually an important part of the healing process. In health and healing, the biochemical effects of brown rice, miso soup, and azuki beans cannot be isolated and analyzed apart from the role of the mind.

Ideally, scientific discoveries should be freely available to everyone, and not used for narrow political or economic gain. At present, the opposite is true. The majority of science graduates in the United States eventually go to work for industry or the defense department. In *Jurassic Park*, the person behind the dinosaur scheme was a businessman, not a scientist. Profit is also the motive behind the recent development of genetically engineered foods.

Scientists have discovered that tomatoes and other vegetables will stay fresh longer if animal genes, such as those of pigs or sheep, are inserted in them. Tomatoes are very yin. They are watery, acidic, high in potassium, and originate in South America. Once picked, they quickly spoil. More yang, hardy vegetables, like squash and onions, keep longer in their natural state. Sheep or pigs are yang in relation to tomatoes and other vegetables. Introducing their more yang genes into vegetables slows the rate at which vegetables spoil, thus increasing "shelf life." However, this practice could easily become nightmarish. Suppose this is done with a staple food such as wheat. If you go to a restaurant and order whole wheat toast, without knowing it, you will be eating animal food. For many people, including ethical vegetarians, such a situation is clearly unacceptable.

The genetic engineering of food has the potential to create chaos in the biological world. It represents humanity's latest assault on the biosphere. The integrity of species is inviolate. Life evolved into its present forms because of the clear distinction between the plant and animal kingdoms. If we we tamper with that distinction, especially on a mass scale, we are threatening the entire network of biorelationships on earth.

Here and there, prophetic voices have warned humanity not to succumb to the illusion that it can control nature. Mary Shelly, in her 19th century classic, *Frankenstein*, tried to show the front and back of scientific attempts to manipulate life. Her point was that if we create monsters, they will come back and destroy us. Shelly knew intuitively that we live in a world of compensation, of yin and yang, or action and reaction. Whatever we do comes back to us. *Jurassic Park* offers a modern version of that same message.

Source: This essay is from a lecture at the 1993 Macrobiotic Summer Conference in Poultney, Vermont, and published in *One Peaceful World*, Autumn, 1993.

Resources

One Peaceful World

One Peaceful World is an international information network and friendship society of individuals, families, educational centers, organic farmers, teachers and parents, authors and artists, publishers and business people, and others devoted to the realization of one healthy, peaceful world. Activities include educational and spiritual tours, assemblies and forums, international food aid and development, and publishing. Membership is $30/year for individuals and $50 for families and includes a subscription to the *One Peaceful World Newsletter* and a free book from One Peaceful World Press. For further information, contact:

One Peaceful World
Box 10, Becket, MA 01223
(413) 623–2322
Fax (413) 623–8827

Kushi Institute

The Kushi Institute offers ongoing classes and seminars in macrobiotic cooking, health care, diagnosis, shiatsu and body energy development, and philosophy. Programs include the Way to Health Seminar, a seven-day residential program presented several times a month including hands-on training in macrobiotic cooking and home care, lectures on the philosophy and practice of macrobiotics, and meals prepared by a specially trained cooking staff; the Dynamics of Macrobiotics Program, which offers four- and five-week intensives for individuals who wish to manage their health and daily life at a deeper level; and Michio Kushi Seminars, four- to five-day intensives with Michio on spiritual training, managing destiny, and a new medicine for humanity. Similar leadership training programs are offered at Kushi Institute affiliates in Europe, and through Kushi Institute Extensions in selected cities in North America and abroad.

The Kushi Institute also offers a variety of special programs including an annual Macrobiotic Summer Conference. For information, contact:

Kushi Institute
Box 7, Becket MA, 01223
(413) 623–5741
Fax (413) 623–8827

Edward Esko began macrobiotic studies with Michio Kushi in 1971 and for twenty years has taught macrobiotic philosophy throughout the United States and Canada, as well as in Western and Eastern Europe, South America, and Japan. He has lectured on modern health issues at the United Nations in New York and is on the faculty of the Kushi Institute in Becket, Mass. He is the author of *Healing Planet Earth* and *Notes from the Boundless Frontier* (One Peaceful World Press), and has co-authored or edited several popular books. He lives with his wife, Wendy, and their seven children in the Berkshires.